David & Charlotte Bailey

# FRESH VEGAN KITCHEN

## DELICIOUS RECIPES FOR THE VEGAN & RAW KITCHEN

PAVILION

# FRESH
# VEGAN
# KITCHEN

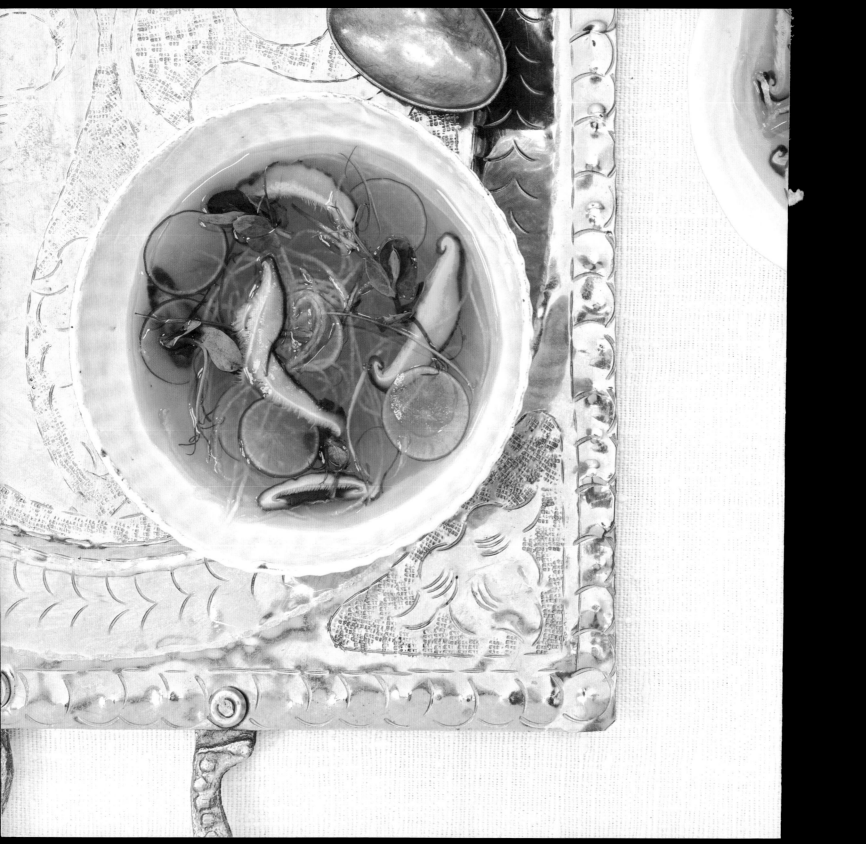

# Contents

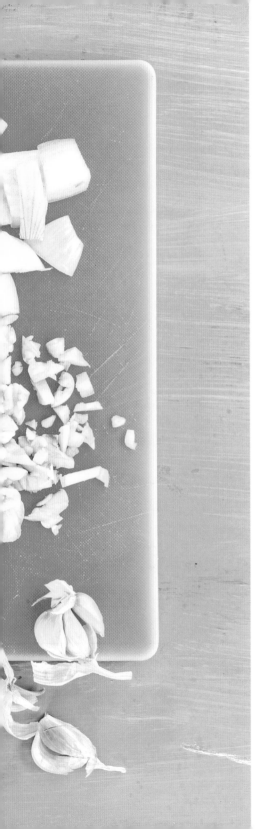

# Introduction

This book is about sharing good food. Yes, these are exclusively recipes that use no animal products, but this food is not about what's missing, but instead about enjoying the extraordinary range of plant-based ingredients that are available.

The arguments for adopting a plant-based diet are persuasive and are gaining momentum every day. Few would counter the assertion that, particularly in the West, we eat far too much meat, both for our own good and for the good of the animals and our planet. The advent of factory farming, the desecration of the rainforests and other natural habitats and the mismanagement of Earth's natural energy resources – as well as the huge increase in diseases such as adult-onset diabetes, allergies, obesity, cancer and heart disease to name but a few – all point to an urgent need to reconsider some of our choices.

For different reasons, more and more people are choosing to embrace a vegan or vegetarian diet. Even more, while not going the whole hog, if you pardon the pun, are deciding to reduce their consumption of animal products. No one way will work for everyone and no matter where we're at, there's always more we could do. But everyone can eat less meat but still eat food that's exciting, vibrant, satisfying and, above all, tastes great.

Most of the recipes in this book are naturally low in saturated fats (aka, the bad fats) and don't use refined ingredients or too much salt or sugar. We've sometimes made suggestions for serving but, if in doubt, add a whole grain, some leafy greens and a handful of nuts or seeds and you'll be well on the road to a satisfying and nutritionally well-rounded meal.

KEY
WF - WHEAT-FREE RECIPE
GF - GLUTEN-FREE RECIPE
RAW - SEE PAGES 9 & 11

Many of our dishes are wheat-free (WF) and gluten-free (GF), and some are also suitable for raw diets – look out for the symbols next to each recipe. If you're able to, use organic ingredients – they are likely to taste better, look better, and be better for you – and they are better for the ecology of the planet.

The cuisines of countries with a long tradition of vegetarianism, particularly in Asia, have provided rich pickings for inspiration. We love to travel and have taken something away from every country we've been to. We hope that you'll enjoy mixing cuisines and experimenting with some more unusual ingredients. Even less well-known ingredients are increasingly available in large supermarkets, and the rest should be easily found in your local health-food shop and Asian grocery or, if needs be, online.

Spanish tapas, Middle Eastern mezze, Indian thali or Chinese dim sum are all inspirations, and this book features lots of little plates of different dishes that complement one another. Of course, we sometimes can't resist mixing styles and combining dishes that you wouldn't normally expect to see together, but this adds up to dynamic and unpredictable eating that brings out the best of vegan cookery. Experimenting is where cooking, and especially vegan cooking, really starts to become fun!

# Health benefits of raw food

Food in its raw state provides optimal nutrition because it contains more essential enzymes than food that has been cooked. These enzymes are considered to be the life-force of food, and offer manifold heath benefits that are greatly reduced if the food is heated over 46°C/115°F, the temperature at which the natural enzymes are destroyed.

Enzymes help you to digest food and are the catalyst for every metabolic reaction in your body. Metabolic reactions are chemical processes, such as cell division, brain activity and energy production; they occur in all living organisms and are essential to maintaining life. They activate hormones and vitamins, enabling them to do their job and strengthen the immune system, among many other things.

Every food contains the perfect mix of enzymes to digest that food completely, but if those enzymes are destroyed through cooking, our bodies are forced to generate their own enzymes to facilitate digestion. This is not desirable because the enzymes produced by the body (digestive enzymes) are not as perfectly combined to digest that food as the enzymes contained within the food itself (food enzymes). This can lead to the food being only partially digested and thus clogging up your intestinal tract and arteries and causing all manor of ailments.

Even more pertinently, the quantity of enzymes the body can produce diminishes with time and the more pressure put on them as a result of the innate enzymes within the food being destroyed, the more the reserve is depleted until there's not much left and ill health ensues.

There are few things more inspiring than a market full of colourful, freshly picked fruit and vegetables, and good raw food is one of the best ways to honour them. The raw diet is also focused around green leafy vegetables, nuts, seeds, sprouts and fresh fruits. All these are incredibly alkalizing and so greatly aid the cleansing process, help to alleviate a number of common ailments and facilitate greater balance. This is important because our Western diets are generally overloaded with very acidic foods, such as sugar, alcohol, meat and most dairy products. We've also included some fermented foods and a 'how to' of sprouting (p.166), as these are foods that are in their growth stage and so at their most nutritious. A few favourite 'superfoods', much beloved by raw foodists, such as lacuma, maca and raw cacao are also included for their amazing nutritional properties

You'll find plenty of raw recipes in this book. In some we use a tiny amounts of special ingredients, such as maple syrup, balsamic vinegar or toasted sesame oil, that aren't strictly speaking raw, but as long as it's a tiny fraction and really adds something to the dish, we think it's okay.

There is always great debate as to whether a fully raw diet is desirable, but few would argue that incorporating more whole and unadulterated plant-based foods into our diets is a bad thing. Many people report better digestion, weight loss, greater energy, clearer skin, incredible healing from disease and many other benefits but we'll leave you to look into the research and make your own decisions as to how far you want to go with it.

# Vegan cooking tips

To get the best results from a culinary point of view, we recommend using a super-sharp knife; it's safer and you'll prevent your food from being bruised and torn and from prematurely oxidising. In raw food recipes, in particular, you want your ingredients to look sharp and full of life and a good blade is essential for this. A spiralizer and a mandolin are relatively inexpensive and will help you make really good-looking raw noodles and ribbons that will spruce up many dishes. As ever, a decent food processor will also be sure to make your life easier!

If you're getting serious, we would go on to recommend a high-powered blender such as a Vitamix, as you really do need the extra horsepower to make nut bases into smooth 'creams' and 'cheeses', and it enables you to turn pretty much any fruit or vegetable into a smooth liquid while maintaining all of its fibre. A dehydrator, too, opens up a whole new realm of possibilities, enhancing flavours and enabling different textures, but both these items are very expensive and we think only worth investing in once you're sure you're committed to this way of eating.

To make the necessary forward planning a bit easier, we always recommend soaking any nuts and seeds you intend to use before you go to bed and then they'll be ready for the next day. Once you get into the habit of planning ahead, you'll develop a routine and find that it isn't as challenging as it might seem at first. It's well worth persevering.

BREAKFASTS

MAKES 1
SANDWICH

# TLT sandwich

When you ask people who have given up meat if there's anything they really miss, bacon always seems to feature in their responses, but this recipe might just help. The tofu does a pretty good job of giving off that distinctive, sweet and smoky aroma that draws people in – and it tastes delicious! It certainly isn't packed full of saturated fat, either, and might actually help to reduce LDL cholesterol. This is a great brunch for lazy mornings.

1 tbsp coconut oil (or cooking oil of your choice)

100g/3½oz/⅓ block smoked tofu, thinly sliced

2 thick slices of bread (we love it with a good sourdough)

1 tbsp vegan mayonnaise

1 tsp wholegrain mustard

2–3 leaves romaine lettuce, washed and shredded

2 tbsp Sauerkraut (p.148)

1 plum tomato, thinly sliced

a few sprigs fresh flat-leaf parsley

salt and pepper

**1** Heat the coconut oil in a frying pan over a medium-high heat. Add the tofu slices and fry for a few minutes until both sides are really crisp.

**2** Lightly toast the bread slices and spread the mayonnaise on one piece and the mustard on the other.

**3** Put the lettuce on top of the mayonnaise, followed by the Sauerkraut, tomato slices, parsley and finally the crispy tofu. Season to taste with salt and pepper and close the sandwich with the other slice of bread. Slice in half and enjoy!

# Scrambled tofu

Another brilliant brunch, this is a straightforward dish that will quickly become a staple in the arsenal of any vegan diet. It makes a great base recipe but is also very easy to modify to your personal preferences by adding different herbs, spices or vegetables. We love it on sourdough with some sautéed potatoes, roasted cherry tomatoes and one or two field mushrooms roasted in the oven with a little olive oil and chopped garlic. If you're really pushing the boat out, a drizzle of good-quality white truffle oil is a big winner! Nutritional yeast is a great source of protein and other nutrients. You can buy it in flakes from health-food stores.

350g/12oz/1 block fresh firm tofu
1 tbsp olive oil
½ onion, finely chopped
1 tsp brown sugar
3 tbsp nutritional yeast (make sure it's gluten free)
salt and pepper

**1** Crumble the tofu with your fingers so that it already starts to resemble scrambled eggs.

**2** Heat the olive oil in a frying pan over a low heat and sauté the onion with a little salt for about 4 minutes, stirring occasionally, until the onion is soft and translucent. Add the brown sugar and continue to heat for a couple of minutes, stirring occasionally, until the onion begins to caramelize.

**3** Add the crumbled tofu, turn the heat up to full blast and cook for 5 minutes or until the tofu starts to dry out, breaking it up with a wooden spoon as it cooks.

**4** Add the nutritional yeast and stir well to combine, then continue to cook until the mixture is totally dry and beginning to catch on the bottom of the pan – this should take another 5 minutes or so and by this point the mixture should look a lot like well-done scrambled eggs. Season to taste with salt and pepper and serve.

MAKES
400ML/
14FL OZ
WF | GF

# Coconut yogurt

This stuff is fantastic and is absolutely brilliant if you're missing yogurt; to our mind it's actually far more delicious and it's a great way of getting probiotics, which equal a happy stomach, clearer skin and a boosted immune system. What's not to love? You will need some probiotics to get you started (look for a vegan powder in your health-food stores or buy gelatine-free capsules and empty them). Once you've made your first batch, you can make the next one simply by stirring a generous spoonful of the finished coconut yogurt into some new coconut milk and the probiotics from the earlier batch will start the process again – easy peasy! We love this served with fresh fruit and some G'raw'nola (p.23). You can also add your choice of sweetener or a swirl of jam or coulis.

400ml/14fl oz/generous 1½ cups coconut milk (full fat and with as few extra stabilisers, preservatives, etc., as possible)

½ tsp probiotic powder

**1** Chill the coconut milk in the fridge for 2–3 hours, which hardens the cream and makes it easier to separate. If you like a thicker yogurt you can scoop off the thicker cream and just use that part (discarding the rest or saving it to use in drinks and sauces). If you are happy with a looser yogurt you can use the whole can.

**2** Sterilize a 500ml (18fl oz) glass jar by pouring boiling water in it; place a metal spoon in it before doing so to avoid cracking the glass. Put the coconut milk and the probiotic powder in and mix thoroughly. Seal the jar.

**3** Leave the jar in a warm place, but away from direct sunlight, for 12–36 hours; the timing will depend on the temperature and time of year, but you'll know it's ready when it resembles the consistency and slightly sour taste of dairy yogurt. (It's important to check on the yogurt regularly during the process, because it can become much too sour, or even go off, if you leave it out too long after the probiotics have done their stuff.)

**4** When the yogurt is ready, transfer to the fridge, where it will continue to thicken the longer you leave it. The yogurt should last about 5 days in an airtight container or covered bowl – if you don't eat it all first!

MAKES 4 SLICES

# 'Eggy' bread

French toast, pain perdu or good old eggy bread – whatever you call it, this is a perfect Sunday treat to enjoy with a pot of coffee while you read the papers. Egg-replacer powder is something we find very useful and is readily available from health-food stores. It is a mixture of arrowroot, baking powder and xanthan gum, which replace the starch, leavening and emulsifying properties that would otherwise be contributed by an egg.

1 tbsp egg-replacer powder

125ml/4fl oz/½ cup Soya Milk, homemade (p.157) or store-bought

1 tbsp maple syrup, plus extra to drizzle

a pinch of freshly grated nutmeg

a pinch of ground cinnamon

1 tbsp coconut oil (or cooking oil of your choice), plus extra for frying, if needed

4 slices of brown bread, white bread or baguette (French bread)

**To serve**

1 batch sweet Raw Cashew Cream (p.141) (optional)

200g/7oz/1⅓ cups mixed berries (strawberries, raspberries, blueberries and blackberries)

icing (confectioners') sugar to dust

1 Put the egg-replacer powder in a large bowl. Add the milk, maple syrup and spices and mix well until smooth.

2 Heat the coconut oil in a frying pan over a medium heat. Quickly dip one slice of bread into the 'egg' mixture and turn until well coated. Add to the pan and fry for 3–4 minutes until well browned, then flip over and brown the other side. Remove from the pan and keep it warm while you repeat with the remaining slices, adding more oil to the pan as needed.

3 Divide onto plates and top with a spoonful of Raw Cashew Cream, if you like. Drizzle with extra maple syrup and add a good handful of berries, then dust with icing sugar and serve.

# Coconut milk porridge

## with bananas, blueberries and maple syrup

This easy switch from milk to coconut milk makes porridge so much more creamy and special. Served with blueberries, maple syrup and a generous handful of mixed seeds, it's also a really nutritious, antioxidant-packed way to start the day. There is some debate as to whether oats are suitable for those on a wheat- and gluten-free diet as there is often cross-contamination, but you can buy oats that are specially labelled as being suitable for free-from diets, or substitute them for another grain – millet is hugely underappreciated and works really well.

1 litre/34fl oz/1 quart water

a pinch of salt

180g/6¼oz/scant 2 cups porridge oats or millet flakes

240ml/8fl oz/1 cup coconut milk

**To serve**

250g/9oz/1⅔ cups blueberries

2 bananas, sliced

50g/2oz/heaped ⅓ cup mixed seeds (chia, sesame, sunflower, linseed, poppy seed)

a little maple syrup

**1** Bring the water to the boil in a large pan, then add the salt and the oats or millet. Bring back to the boil, then reduce the heat and simmer for a further 10 minutes, stirring continuously, until the porridge has a nice creamy consistency.

**2** Stir in the coconut milk and return to the boil. Divide the porridge into bowls and serve sprinkled with blueberries, banana slices and seeds, and with a small jug of maple syrup for drizzling over the top.

MAKES
ABOUT
1.7KG/4LB
WF | GF | RAW
OPTION

# G'raw'nola

This is super-quick and easy and makes a delicious breakfast or any-time-of-the-day snack served with fresh fruit and Coconut Yogurt (p.19). The mixture is very moist, so you can also easily shape it into bars for portable snacks – these are especially good dipped in melted dark or raw chocolate. Raw chocolate is available in health food stores and unlike processed dark chocolate it hasn't been heated, so it keeps all its good nutrition intact. To keep this recipe raw, you really need a dehydrator, but you can make a baked version of the recipe if you don't have one. If you do use an oven, you don't need to soak the nuts and seeds first, as this is done to germinate them, the benefit of which will only remain if the mix is kept raw. The mixture will last for several weeks in an airtight container.

250g/9oz/2 cups sunflower seed kernels

200g/7oz/generous 1 cup buckwheat

250g/9oz/2½ cups pecans

250g/9oz/2 cups walnuts

125g/4½oz/1 cup pumpkin seeds

250g/9oz/2 cups dried apricots, chopped

125g/4½oz/1 cup dried cranberries, chopped

50g/1¾oz/½ cup desiccated coconut

1 apple, grated

200g/7oz/1⅓ cups medjool dates, pitted

2 tbsp agave syrup, maple syrup or sweetener of your choice

2 tbsp lemon juice

1 tbsp ground cinnamon

½ tbsp freshly grated nutmeg

1 tbsp vanilla extract

**1** To make the recipe using an oven, preheat the oven to 160°C/325°F/gas mark 3.

**2** Mix together all the ingredients, then spread them on a baking sheet and bake for 25–30 minutes until golden brown, stirring and turning the mixture every 10 minutes or so and keeping a close eye on it to make sure it doesn't burn. Leave to cool, then store in an airtight container.

**3** To make the recipe in a dehydrator, soak the sunflower seed kernels, buckwheat, pecans, walnuts and pumpkin seeds in water for 8 hours.

**4** Drain the soaked ingredients, then mix them with all the remaining ingredients in a food processor.

**5** Loosely spread the mixture on Teflex sheets, set the dehydrator to 45°C/113°F and dehydrate the sheets for about 24 hours, moving the mixture around every 6 hours or so. Store in an airtight container.

SERVES 2
WF | GF
RAW
OPTION

# Acai bowl

This is a brilliant healthy start to the day and it's beautiful to behold as well. Acai (ah-sah-EE) bowls are a traditional Brazilian breakfast that have become something of a trend, especially in Hawaii and LA. As the name suggests, they're focused around puréed acai berries – the dark-purple fruit of the acai palm tree, native to the Amazonian regions of Brazil. They're absolutely delicious, with a taste redolent of dark chocolate, and are also laden with antioxidants, amino acids and essential fatty acids – so it's no wonder they've gained superfood status! Alongside the acai purée, you can add whatever you like, but granola, bananas, other berries and a sweetener of some kind are the usual suspects. The acai needs to be bought in pulp form and you'll find this in the freezer section of health-food stores. If you can't find it, this is still a fab breakfast if you substitute the acai with the same amount of frozen berries.

### For the acai purée

200g/7oz frozen acai purée

1 banana

2 medjool dates, pitted

125ml/4fl oz/½ cup apple juice, coconut water or Almond Milk, homemade (p.157) or store-bought

1 tbsp hemp or chia seeds (optional)

### Toppings

2 handfuls of mixed berries

1 banana, sliced

a handful of desiccated coconut

a small handful of dried goji berries, mulberries, cranberries or raw cacao nibs

200g/7oz raw G'raw'nola (p.23) or your favourite granola

sweetener of your choice (agave or coconut palm nectar or maple syrup) (optional)

fresh mint leaves to garnish (optional)

**1** Put the frozen acai, banana, dates, apple juice and seeds, if using, in a blender or food processor and blend until smooth.

**2** Divide the purée between two bowls and sprinkle over your choice of toppings. Garnish with mint leaves, if you like, and serve.

# Black rice pudding

SERVES 4
WF | GF

This classic Balinese dish, known as bubur injin, is served all day long as a breakfast, an in-between snack or as a dessert in its home country. Its glossy black looks, punctuated with a swirl of creamy white coconut milk, have captivated many a heart, and it has become a firm favourite in our household. Black glutinous rice is readily available in Asian supermarkets. The pandan leaf can be a little bit trickier to find and is definitely not a necessity, but if you can track it down it does add a unique South East Asian taste to proceedings. If serving as a dessert, a scoop or two of vegan ice cream works very well!

300g/10½oz/1½ cups black glutinous rice, washed

1½ litres/52fl oz/1½ quarts water, plus extra to soak

1 pandan leaf (optional)

90g/3¼oz/½ cup palm sugar

4 tbsp desiccated coconut

450ml/16fl oz/scant 2 cups coconut milk

a pinch of salt

2 bananas, sliced diagonally

**1** Cover the black rice with water and leave to soak overnight.

**2** Drain and rinse the rice, then drain again. Put it in a saucepan with the water and pandan leaf, if using. Bring to the boil over a high heat, then reduce the heat to medium and cook for 25–30 minutes, or until the rice is nice and tender. Stir in the sugar and cook for a further 5 minutes, then remove from the heat and set aside.

**3** Meanwhile, lightly toast the desiccated coconut in a dry frying pan over a medium heat for a few minutes until golden, shaking the pan frequently. Remove the coconut from the pan and set aside.

**4** In another pan, bring the coconut milk and salt to the boil over a medium heat, then simmer until reduced by about one-third.

**5** Divide the black rice into four bowls and swirl one-quarter of the coconut milk into each one. Serve topped with banana slices and a sprinkle of toasted coconut.

SOUPS

# Laksa

A wonderful main-meal soup, laksa is a mouth-watering, highly aromatic coconut-curry broth filled with noodles and, in this version, tofu puffs and an assortment of vegetables. It's usually very spicy, designed to make you sweat (and hence keep cool) as you eat it by the roadside in the tropics, but you can moderate the chilli according to your taste and climate.

200g/7oz dried rice noodles

4 tbsp coconut oil (or cooking oil of your choice)

2 tbsp palm sugar

1 batch Laksa Curry Paste (p.170)

400ml/14fl oz/1¾ cups coconut milk

1 batch Laksa Vegetable Stock (p.170)

1–2 tsp tamari (make sure it's gluten free)

150g/5½oz/1 heaped cup mangetout (snow peas), cut in half

125g/4½oz/½ cup baby corn, cut in half lengthways

150g/5½oz/1 cup enoki mushrooms

2 red chillies, deseeded and thinly sliced

100g/3½oz/scant ⅓ block tofu puffs or marinated tofu pieces

1 bunch of fresh coriander (cilantro), plus extra to sprinkle

1 bunch of fresh Thai basil, picked

250g/9oz/1⅔ cups cherry tomatoes, halved

a handful of Crispy Fried Shallots (green onions) (p.48) or crispy fried Thai shallots (p.74)

large lime wedges to serve

salt and pepper

**1** Soak the rice noodles in a bowl of water for about 1 hour, then drain.

**2** In a large pan, heat the coconut oil, then add the palm sugar and Laksa Curry Paste and continue to cook, stirring occasionally, for about 10 minutes until it starts to brown and caramelize. Add the coconut milk and stock and bring to the boil, then reduce the heat and simmer for a further 20 minutes. Season with tamari to taste, then strain.

**3** Return the soup to the pan and slowly bring up to the boil, adding the mangetout, baby corn, enoki mushrooms, red chillies and tofu puffs or pieces as it heats up. Meanwhile, take 4 large bowls and divide the soaked rice noodles, herbs and cherry tomatoes among them. As the soup comes up to the boil, reduce to a simmer, then check the seasoning and add a little more tamari, if needed.

**4** Pour the soup over the noodles and vegetables. Sprinkle with extra coriander leaves and crispy shallots and serve with lime wedges for squeezing over.

# Tom yum hed soup

SERVES 4
WF | GF

Tom yum hed is a spicy, clear soup eaten throughout South East Asia and distinguished by its hot, sour flavour. 'Tom' refers to the boiling process, 'yum' (or yam, as it's sometimes known) refers to a spicy and sour Thai salad, and 'hed' means mushroom. Serve with the lemongrass, galangal and lime leaves still in – but don't eat them! It's best to eat tom yum hed as soon as you've made it, as the flavours can become overpowering and bitter when left to infuse for too long.

1 batch Asian Vegetable Stock (p.169)

15g/½oz galangal, peeled and roughly chopped

4 kaffir lime leaves

1 stick lemongrass, sliced

1–3 long red chillies, deseeded and sliced (depending on how spicy you like it!)

1 tsp palm sugar

10g/¼oz coriander root, roughly chopped

100g/3½oz/scant 1 cup mushrooms (oyster, enoki, shimiji or a mix)

80g/3oz/about ½ cup mangetout (snow peas) or fine green beans

10 baby corn, cut in half lengthways

5 cherry tomatoes, halved

a pinch of salt

juice of 1 lime

2 tbsp tamari (make sure it's gluten free)

a large handful of fresh coriander (cilantro) leaves

a handful of fresh Thai basil leaves

1 Put the stock in a large pan and bring to the boil over a high heat. Add the galangal, lime leaves, lemongrass, chillies, palm sugar and coriander root. Reduce the heat to medium and simmer for 5 minutes.

2 Add the mushrooms, mangetout, baby corn and tomatoes and continue to simmer for a couple of minutes.

3 Season with salt, lime juice and tamari – adjust the seasoning to taste but use the quantities in the list of ingredients as a guide. Return the soup to the boil, add the coriander leaves and Thai basil and serve.

# Miso soup

SERVES 4
WF | GF

Traditionally eaten every day for breakfast, miso soup is a real staple of the Japanese diet. It consists of a stock, known as dashi, into which miso paste is added. Dashi is traditionally made using bonito (skipjack tuna) flakes, but for vegans the fishy taste is replicated here by using a combination of seaweeds and shiitake mushrooms. Miso is a paste made from fermented soya beans, so you receive all the digestive benefits of the fermentation process as well as a full whack of antioxidants and fatty acids. It's also particularly helpful for vegans, as the bacteria in miso synthesize vitamin B12, a vital nutrient that is difficult to obtain from a purely plant-based diet. Kombu is also available in health-food stores.

½ head broccoli, cut into very small florets

500ml/17fl oz/generous 2 cups Vegetable Stock, homemade (p.170) or store-bought

1 stick kombu (edible kelp)

2 dried shiitake mushrooms, soaked in water for 4 hours, then drained

1 tbsp gluten-free white miso paste (sometimes known as sweet), plus extra to season

200g/7oz firm silken tofu, cut into small cubes

4 pinches of wakame (edible seaweed)

1 spring onion (scallion), finely shredded, to garnish

**1** Blanch the broccoli florets in a pan of boiling salted water for a minute or so until just tender. Drain, then refresh in a bowl of ice-cold water for 30 seconds. Drain again and set aside.

**2** Put the stock in a large pan with the kombu stick and shiitake mushrooms. Heat until just below boiling point, then remove the kombu and turn off the heat.

**3** Whisk in the white miso paste and taste, adding a little more paste if you feel it's needed, or a little water if it tastes too strong. Return to the heat and add the blanched broccoli florets, tofu and wakame. Gently reheat the soup without boiling (boiling kills the miso's probiotic qualities). When the soup looks pretty hot, garnish with spring onion and serve immediately.

# Rainbow congee

SERVES 2
WF | GF

Congee is a style of rice porridge eaten in many Asian countries, but it is especially popular in China, where its warm, comforting nature makes it a very common meal for convalescents, especially in its plain form. The extra seasonings and garnishes are where this dish becomes colourful and exciting, however, and you can experiment as much as you like with these. We're using white rice, as it's more traditional and gives a smoother finish, but you can substitute your own choice of grain. Short-grained brown rice would work well but you could also try it with millet, sorghum or barley. You should be able to find red dates and candlenuts in good Asian grocery stores; they're delicious in this recipe.

1 batch Asian Vegetable Stock (p.169)

15g/½oz arame (a type of kelp)

1 tsp coconut oil (or cooking oil of your choice)

½ onion, chopped

1 small carrot, diced

8 mangetout (snow peas), diced

200g/7oz/1 cup white long-grain rice

10 candlenuts, quartered (optional)

10 red dates, pitted and sliced (optional)

a large pinch of salt

1 tsp tamari, plus extra to serve (make sure it's gluten free)

a handful of Crispy Fried Shallots (green onions) (p.48) or crispy fried Thai shallots (p.74)

1 spring onion (scallion), finely chopped, to serve

white pepper to serve

1 While the stock is cooking, soak the arame in boiling water for 15–20 minutes, then drain and set aside.

2 Remove the stalks from the reserved stock mushrooms and thinly slice the caps.

3 Heat the coconut oil in a large pan and sauté the onion until translucent. Add the carrot, mangetout and sliced shiitake mushrooms and continue to sauté until the mixture really starts to become aromatic. Turn off the heat and set aside.

4 Put the stock into a large saucepan with the rice, sautéed vegetables, candlenuts and red dates, if using, then add the salt and tamari and bring to the boil. Reduce the heat to low and simmer for 1–1½ hours, stirring occasionally, until the rice has broken up and has a porridge-like texture. (You do need to keep an eye on the soup, especially towards the end of the cooking process, to make sure the mixture doesn't burn on the bottom).

5 Stir in the arame and simmer for a further 5–10 minutes. Spoon into bowls and sprinkle crispy shallots and spring onion over each one. Serve with tamari and white pepper on the side so you can season to taste at the table.

# Corn chowder

SERVES 4
WF | GF
OPTION

A relative of the famous New England clam chowder, this is real comfort food. Chowder is a creamy soup often thickened by the addition of crushed cream crackers. Our dear friend coconut milk lends the creaminess to this corn version, and we think it's naturally thick enough to serve with croûtons rather than crackers.

1 tbsp coconut oil (or cooking oil of your choice)

1 onion, chopped

3 garlic cloves, chopped

½ long red chilli, deseeded and chopped

5 sweetcorn (corn) cobs, kernels shaved off, reserving 2 cobs and a few kernels

1½ carrots, peeled and diced

2 litres/68fl oz/2 quarts Vegetable Stock homemade (p.170) or store-bought

450g/1lb/3 cups new potatoes, roughly chopped

200ml/7fl oz/scant 1 cup coconut milk

salt and pepper

lime wedges to serve

**For the herby croûtons (omit for a wheat- and gluten-free option)**

2 slices of bread, cut into 1cm/½in squares

1 tbsp olive oil

a pinch of dried thyme

a pinch of dried rosemary

**1** Heat the coconut oil in large pan and sauté the onion until translucent. Add the garlic and chilli and continue to sauté for 3–4 minutes, then add the sweetcorn kernels and carrots and sauté for another minute or so.

**2** Next, cut the reserved corn cobs in half. Pour the stock over the sauté mix and add the cob halves and the new potatoes. Bring to the boil, then reduce the heat and simmer for 15–20 minutes, stirring occasionally, until all the vegetables are tender.

**3** While the soup is simmering, make the croûtons. Preheat the oven to 200°C/400°F/gas mark 6. Put the bread in a bowl and toss with the olive oil, thyme and rosemary to coat. Transfer to a baking sheet and bake for 10 minutes until lightly golden, moving the croûtons around the baking sheet every couple of minutes or so. Set aside.

**4** When the soup is ready, remove and discard the corn cobs. Working in batches, transfer one-third of the soup at a time to a blender or food processor and pulse until smooth – be very careful as hot soup can explode. Return the soup to the pan, stir in the coconut milk and reheat for 10–15 minutes over a very low heat.

**5** Season to taste with salt and pepper, then divide into bowls and sprinkle the croûtons over the top. Garnish with the reserved sweetcorn kernels and serve with a wedge of lime for squeezing over.

# Tortilla soup

SERVES 2
WF | GF

The origins of this popular Mexican soup are a bit of a mystery and there are countless variations. People argue ferociously over which version is correct (and best!), but no matter which one you pick you'll enjoy a pungent, deeply comforting mix of heady flavours. It's usually topped with tortillas that are sliced and then toasted, and this adds an unusual toasted-corn element, but you can substitute the tortillas for tortilla chips if you want to save time. In place of soured cream, we've used avocado – a vegan's best friend – for its easy, creamy goodness.

1 onion, chopped

1 tbsp olive oil, plus extra for coating

2 garlic cloves, thinly sliced

2 red (bell) peppers, deseeded and diced

1 courgette (zucchini), diced

2 sweetcorn (corn) cobs, kernels shaved off

½ red chilli, deseeded and chopped

1 chipotle chilli

1 spring onion (scallion), chopped

1 tbsp ground cumin

1 tsp mild smoked paprika

1 tsp salt

½ tsp white pepper

400g/14oz tinned chopped tomatoes

500ml/17fl oz/generous 2 cups Vegetable Stock, homemade (p.170) or store-bought

4 corn tortillas, cut into strips, or ½ bag tortilla chips

400g/14oz tinned mixed beans, drained and rinsed

**To serve**

a few fresh coriander (cilantro) leaves

1 avocado, peeled, stoned and sliced

2 limes, halved

**1** In a large pan, sauté the onion in the olive oil until translucent. Add the garlic, peppers, courgette, sweetcorn kernels, red chilli, chipotle and spring onion. Season with the cumin, paprika, salt and white pepper and stir well. Cook over a low heat for about 10 minutes, then add the chopped tomatoes and the vegetable stock and bring to the boil. Reduce the heat slightly, partially cover and simmer for a further 25–30 minutes.

**2** Meanwhile, prepare the sliced corn tortillas, if using. Preheat the oven to 180°C/350°F/gas mark 4. Coat the tortilla strips with a little olive oil and arrange them in a single layer on a baking tray. Toast in the oven for about 5 minutes, or until nice and crisp. Set aside.

**3** Add the beans to the soup and cook for another 10 minutes until heated through. Check the seasoning and adjust to taste. Divide the soup into bowls and serve topped with coriander, avocado, toasted tortilla strips or chips and a squeeze of lime juice.

# Pepper water

Tangy rasam, or pepper water, is a popular Southern Indian dish and the inspiration for the well-known Anglo-Indian mulligatawny soup. Many people drink a cup of it after a meal, as the spices are considered to aid digestion, but it's also often enjoyed as a simple meal and is delicious served with white rice.

1 tbsp vegetable oil

1 tsp mustard seeds

1 onion, thinly sliced

3 garlic cloves, finely chopped

a handful of curry leaves

1 tsp tamarind paste

4 fresh green peppercorns

a small handful of fresh coriander, roughly chopped

salt and cracked black pepper

**For the stock**

1.5 litres/2½ pints/generous 6 cups water

3 large tomatoes, roughly chopped

1 long red dried chilli, crushed to a powder

1 tsp cumin seeds

½ tsp turmeric

½ tsp coriander seeds, ground

2 tsp vegan bouillon powder

1 To make the stock, put all the stock ingredients in a large pan and bring to the boil. Reduce the heat and simmer for 15–20 minutes until all the vegetables are soft. Leave to cool completely, then pour the stock into a blender or food processor, in batches if necessary, and whiz until smooth.

2 Wipe the pan clean and heat the vegetable oil over a medium-high heat. Add the mustard seeds and cook for 30 seconds until fragrant, then add the onion, garlic and curry leaves and sauté for 2 minutes.

3 Add the tamarind paste, peppercorns and stock and stir well. Bring to the boil, then reduce the heat and simmer for 10 minutes, stirring occasionally until everything is cooked through and well blended. Stir in the coriander leaves, season with salt and cracked black pepper and serve.

# Chilled cucumber and wasabi soup

SERVES 2–4
WF | GF | RAW

This light chilled soup is so quick and easy to make and is brilliantly refreshing on a hot day. We love the tongue-tangling combination of super-cool cucumber and spicy, hot wasabi! It's absolutely delicious served with a few ice cubes floating in the soup.

2 cucumbers, peeled and cut into large chunks

1 avocado, peeled, stoned and halved

2 spring onions (scallions), roughly chopped

2 tsp chopped fresh dill, plus a little extra to garnish

1 tsp wasabi paste (you can add a little more to taste for extra kick! Make sure it's gluten free)

2 handfuls of fresh coriander (cilantro)

250ml/9fl oz/1 generous cup water

a pinch of salt

ice cubes to serve (optional)

**1** Put all the ingredients in a blender or food processor, in batches if necessary, and whiz until smooth.

**2** Transfer to an airtight container and leave to chill in the fridge for at least 2 hours.

**3** Divide the soup into bowls, add a few ice cubes to each one, if you like, and serve.

# Raw shiitake 'noodle' broth

This light and delicate raw soup is extremely refreshing, especially when served chilled. The star of the show is the shiitake, long revered throughout Asia not just as a delicious ingredient but as a vital part of traditional medicine thanks to its ability to enhance immune function and other health boosting benefits.

5 dried shiitake mushrooms

1 litre/34fl oz/1 quart water

1 tbsp rice wine vinegar (brown if possible)

1–2 tsp tamari (make sure it's gluten free)

1 tsp lemon juice

6 radishes

6 mangetout

100g/3½oz daikon (aka mooli or white radish), cut in batons or spirals to resemble noodles

1 tbsp chopped spring onion (scallions), green part only, to garnish

micro-herbs (mizuna, radish, celery or whatever you can find) to garnish

**1** Soak the shiitake mushrooms in the water for 4 hours, then strain and set aside, reserving the soaking water in a bowl – this will be the basis of the broth.

**2** Season the broth with the rice wine vinegar, tamari to taste and lemon juice. If you would like to serve the broth chilled, transfer the water to the fridge for about 30 minutes, then continue with step 3.

**3** Cut the radishes, mangetout and 4 of the soaked shiitake mushrooms into thin slices, then add to the broth with the daikon. Divide into bowls and garnish with the spring onion greens and micro-herbs of your choice. Chop the remaining shiitake mushroom and sprinkle on top to serve.

# Raw borsht

SERVES 2
WF | GF
RAW

There is fierce debate as to where this popular beetroot soup originated, and attributing it to any one country can potentially cause great offence. Nevertheless, it is certainly most popular throughout Eastern Europe, where its hearty nature and rich, vibrant colour soothe the senses and pack a big nutritional punch no matter what the regional variation or whether it's served hot or cold.

1 beetroot (beet), roughly chopped
1 celery stick, roughly chopped
¼ onion, roughly chopped
¼ lemon, roughly chopped
100g/3½oz cabbage, roughly chopped
10g/¼oz fresh root ginger, peeled and roughly chopped
¼ tsp apple cider vinegar
a pinch of salt
a pinch of cracked black pepper

**To serve**
1 batch sour Raw Cashew Cream (p.141) (optional)
a handful of pea shoots

**1** Put all the ingredients in a blender or food processor. Blend on the fastest setting, adding water as needed to reach a smooth, thick consistency.

**2** Divide into bowls and serve with a swirl of sour Raw Cashew Cream, if you like, and some pea shoots.

# Watermelon gazpacho

SERVES 4
WF | GF | RAW

It's taken us a while to fully embrace cold soups (generally our climate is rather better suited to steaming hot broths) but we do have occasional sweltering days and this is a perfect recipe to celebrate them with. As far as chilled soups go, gazpacho is surely the king and the watermelon is a wonderful twist that brings a lovely sweetness and elevates it to another level of refreshing. It's summer in a bowl and so easy to understand why the Spanish say 'de gazpacho no hay empacho' to mean you can never get enough of a good thing!

350g/12oz/scant 1½ cups firm, ripe tomatoes, roughly chopped

350g/12oz watermelon, deseeded and cut into chunks

2 spring onions (scallions), roughly chopped

1 garlic clove, crushed

1 cucumber, roughly chopped

1 red (bell) pepper, deseeded and roughly chopped

1 tsp chopped fresh basil

4 tbsp cold-pressed olive oil

1½ tsp sherry vinegar

100–250ml/3½–9fl oz or ½–1 cup water

ice cubes

salt and pepper

**For the garnish**

2 spring onions (scallions), finely chopped

1 tbsp finely chopped fresh parsley

a few fresh mint leaves

**1** Put the tomatoes, watermelon, spring onions and garlic into a blender or food processor. Add half the cucumber and half the red pepper, then add the basil, olive oil and sherry vinegar and season with salt and pepper.

**2** Blend until smooth, then add the water, a little at a time, until the soup has thinned slightly. Blend again and transfer to the fridge to chill thoroughly for at least 2 hours.

**3** Meanwhile, chop the remaining cucumber and pepper more finely.

**4** Divide the soup into bowls, add a few ice cubes to each one, then sprinkle some red pepper and cucumber over the top. Garnish with spring onions, parsley and mint leaves and serve.

SMALL
PLATES &
STREET
FOOD

# Gyoza dumplings (pot stickers)
## with black vinegar dipping sauce

These crescent-shaped dumplings are one of our all-time favourites. They're called 'pot stickers' in North America, because the traditional and best method of cooking them results in them sticking to the bottom of the pan. Don't worry: they're easy to remove with a spatula, and this technique will give you a wonderful juxtaposition of crispiness on the bottom with fluffiness on the top. You'll find the skins in the freezer section of Asian supermarkets, but do make sure they're vegan because not all varieties are.

**For the dipping sauce**

4 tbsp soy sauce

2 tbsp mirin

2 tsp toasted sesame oil

3½ tbsp rice vinegar

1 shallot (green onion), finely chopped

½ bunch of fresh chives, finely chopped

1 red chilli, deseeded and finely chopped

**For the dumplings**

4 tbsp vegetable oil

1 onion, chopped

1 garlic clove, crushed

15g/½oz fresh root ginger, peeled and finely chopped

1 red chilli, deseeded and finely chopped

2 carrots, grated

1 bunch of spring onions (scallions), finely chopped

3 wood ear mushrooms (or any mushroom of your choice), finely sliced

350g/12oz fresh firm tofu

1 tbsp soy sauce

1 tbsp toasted sesame oil

400g/12oz pack dumpling skins

**1** To make the sauce, combine all the ingredients in a bowl and set aside.

**2** For the dumpling filling, heat 1 tbsp of the vegetable oil in a pan, then add the onion, garlic, ginger and chilli and sauté for about 4 minutes until cooked through. Add the carrot, spring onions and mushrooms, then crumble the tofu into the pan. Cook the mixture for 10–15 minutes until it's quite dry, then season with the soy sauce and toasted sesame oil. Leave until cool enough to handle.

**3** Take a dumpling skin in one hand, then dip the index finger of your other hand in a little water and use it to wet the top half of the skin. Put about ½ tbsp of the filling mixture into the middle of the skin, then fold the skin over to form a half-moon shape, crimping and sticking the edges together as you go. Repeat with the remaining skins and filling.

**4** In a large frying pan with a lid, heat the remaining vegetable oil over a high heat. Add the dumplings to the pan and fry, uncovered, for about 4 minutes until the bottoms are golden and crisp.

**5** Add a ladleful of water and quickly put the lid on the frying pan to steam the dumplings for 2 minutes. Remove the lid and continue to fry, uncovered, until any leftover water has evaporated – be careful as the hot liquid can splash. Keep an eye on the bottom of the dumplings at this stage as you don't want them to burn. Gently lift the dumplings with a spatula and transfer them to a serving plate and serve immediately with the dipping sauce.

# Salt and pepper oyster mushrooms

Deep-fried salt and pepper dishes are a staple of many Chinese restaurants and they're very hard to resist! These oyster mushrooms make a delicious snack covered with crispy garlic, shallots and chilli, but you can also serve them with rice and greens as part of a larger meal. We use oyster mushrooms a lot for their meaty texture, and they work really well in this dish in place of the more commonly used chicken. You'll also find we use the Crispy Fried Shallots in several recipes throughout the book.

### For the Crispy Fried Shallots

500ml/17fl oz/generous 2 cups vegetable oil

5 small shallots (green onions), thinly sliced

### For the rest

3 garlic cloves, chopped

2 long red chillies, deseeded and thinly sliced

125g/4½oz/scant 1½ cups oyster mushrooms, torn into strips

50g/1¾oz/heaped ⅓ cup cornflour (cornstarch)

1 spring onion (scallion), green part only, very thinly sliced

salt and pepper

**1** Put the oil in a wok or large saucepan and heat to about 160°C/325°F, or until a small piece of bread sizzles and turns golden within 20 seconds. Add the shallots to the pan and stir gently, watching closely for the first signs of them turning golden (this should take a couple of minutes). As soon as the shallots start to change colour, carefully remove them from the oil using a small sieve. Drain on kitchen paper (paper towels), sprinkle with salt and leave to cool.

**2** Check the temperature of the oil and turn off the heat if it has become too hot. When the oil is back to 160°C/325°F, prepare the garlic in exactly the same way.

**3** Check the temperature of the oil again, then deep-fry the chillies – as they are a little more prone to burning, we find it easier to deep-fry them in a small sieve, dipping them in and out of the oil until they show the very first signs of going crispy.

**4** Bring the oil up to 200°C/400°F. In a bowl, toss the mushrooms in the cornflour until they're completely coated. Working in batches, shake off any excess cornflour and deep-fry half of the mushrooms, stirring them occasionally with a spoon. When they start to look nice and crispy, remove them from the oil with a slotted spoon. Drain on kitchen paper and season generously with salt and pepper. Repeat with the remaining batch.

**5** Transfer the mushrooms to a plate, sprinkle over the garlic, chilli, shallots and spring onion and serve.

# Bean curd rolls

MAKES 12

Bean curd is a great source of protein and provides the perfect crispy coating for the soft, stir-fried filling. You should be able to find ready-made skins in most Asian supermarkets, but it's fun (if a little time-consuming) to make them from scratch using homemade Soya Milk (p.157).

2 tbsp vegetable oil, plus extra to deep-fry

1 carrot, grated

200g/7oz bean sprouts

300g/10½oz/scant 1 block firm tofu, drained and cut into thin strips

4 dried shiitake mushrooms, soaked in water for 4 hours, then drained and cut into thin strips

8 button mushrooms, sliced

5 tinned water chestnuts, drained, rinsed and sliced

100g/3½oz tinned bamboo shoots, cut into thin strips

a pinch of salt

a pinch of sugar

2 spring onions (scallions), finely sliced

1 tbsp tamari

1 tsp toasted sesame oil

1 tbsp plain (all-purpose) flour

red rice wine vinegar, for dipping

**For the bean curd skins**

1 litre/34fl oz/1 quart Soya Milk, homemade (p.157) or store-bought

**1** To make the bean curd skins, preheat the oven to 80°C/175°F/gas mark ½ and line 2–3 baking sheets with greaseproof (waxed) paper.

**2** In a large wide pan, heat the soya milk until just below boiling point and simmer for about 10 minutes, adjusting the heat so the milk doesn't cool down or boil madly, until a skin begins to form on the surface. Take two chopsticks and very gently place them underneath the skin and carefully transfer it to a prepared baking sheet, trying to keep it intact. Transfer the baking sheet to the oven and leave the skin to dry out for about 20 minutes. Repeat the process until you have enough skins to make twelve 15 x 18cm/6 x 7in rectangles.

**3** Place a wok on a high heat. Add the vegetable oil and when it is very hot, stir-fry the carrot, bean sprouts and tofu for about 1 minute, then throw in the mushrooms, water chestnuts and bamboo shoots and toss everything together. Add the salt, sugar and spring onions and stir-fry for a further minute. Add the tamari and sesame oil and toss again. Remove the mixture from the wok, then drain off any excess liquid and leave to cool.

**4** In a small bowl, combine the flour with a little water to make a smooth paste. Next, peel off a sheet of bean curd and trim with a sharp knife to make a 15 x 18cm/6 x 7in rectangle. Place 2 tbsp of the filling at one end and roll into a parcel, tucking the sides in as you go. Brush the end of the roll with the flour paste to seal, then repeat with the remaining ingredients.

**5** Add enough oil to fill the wok one-quarter full and heat to 180°C/355°F, or until a small piece of bread sizzles and turns golden within 60 seconds. Working in batches, deep-fry the rolls for 4 minutes until golden. Remove with a slotted spoon and drain on kitchen paper (paper towels). Serve with a bowl of red rice wine vinegar for dipping.

# Bao zi steamed buns

MAKES ABOUT 14–16

Bao zi, bao, pau, humbow, bausak … these Chinese steamed buns go by many names and are a key part of any dim sum. They may look tricky, but are straightforward once you know how. Try them with Sunomono (p.117).

**For the dough**

3 tbsp sugar

2 tsp quick yeast

280ml/9½fl oz/1¼ cups warm water

2 tbsp vegetable oil, plus a little extra

500g/1lb 2oz/4 cups plain (all-purpose) flour

2 tbsp cornflour (cornstarch)

2 tsp baking powder

½ tsp salt

**For the filling**

800g/1lb 12oz bok choy

2 tbsp vegetable oil

1 onion, finely chopped

5 spring onions (scallions), finely sliced

1 garlic clove, finely chopped

50g/1¾oz/½ cup dried shiitake mushrooms, soaked in water for 4 hours, then drained and diced

2 tbsp soy sauce

2 tsp sesame oil

½ tsp salt

½ tsp white pepper

**To serve**

1 batch Miso Dipping Sauce (p.168)

**1** To make the dough, dissolve the sugar and yeast in the warm water. Leave to one side for about 10 minutes until the mixture becomes bubbly. Add the oil, then sift the flour, cornflour and baking powder into a bowl and add the salt. Pour the yeast mixture into the bowl and mix to a dough. Knead the dough for about 10 minutes, or until it has formed a nice non-sticky ball. Transfer to an oiled metal bowl, cover with damp kitchen paper (paper towels) and leave to rest in a warm place for about 45 minutes until the dough has more than doubled in size.

**2** Meanwhile, to make the filling, bring a pan of water to the boil. Blanch the bok choy for 2–3 minutes, then drain and refresh with ice-cold water. Pat dry and finely chop. Heat the oil in a wok over a high heat and sauté the onion for a couple of minutes. Add the spring onions and garlic and cook over a medium heat for a further 2 minutes, then add the mushrooms and continue cooking until fragrant. Transfer to a bowl, add the remaining filling ingredients and mix well.

**3** Knead the dough into a neat round and divide into 14–16 equal portions (about 50g/2oz each). Roll each one into a ball and place on a tray lined with clingfilm (plastic wrap). Loosely cover with more clingfilm and leave to rise for a further 30 minutes.

**4** Using the palm of your hand or a rolling pin, shape each ball into a flat disc. Put a teaspoonful of the filling in the centre of each disc, then enclose it by folding the edges of the dough towards the middle. Seal the centres.

**5** Line a bamboo or metal steamer with greaseproof (waxed) paper. Add as many buns as you can comfortably fit and steam for about 10 minutes, or until the buns are light and fluffy. Repeat with the remaining batches. Serve the buns piping hot with a side of Miso Dipping Sauce.

# Cambodian wedding day dip

SERVES 2
WF | GF
OPTION

We discovered this dish on our first wedding anniversary, so it was very appropriate! We'd just arrived in Siem Reap, and due to the prevalence of fish sauce and shrimp paste in everything, hadn't had a particularly good meal for some time. We asked the manager of our hotel where we should eat that night and without even knowing we were vegetarian, he recommended a veggie place in town. It was so amazing that we ate there every night, and by our final evening we had plucked up the courage to ask how this dish, our favourite, was made. They were so generous in giving us the recipe and, with a few tweaks and more easily available ingredients, here it is! It's so easy to make and is a lovely dish to share.

1½ tbsp vegetable oil

250g/9oz/2¾ cups oyster mushrooms, chopped

2 tbsp palm sugar

50g/1¾oz yellow curry paste (make sure it's gluten free)

2 tbsp chilli paste

300ml/10½fl oz/scant 1½ cups coconut milk

50g/1¾oz/⅓ cup roasted peanuts, crushed

salt and pepper

**To serve**

1–2 spring onions (scallions), cut into julienne strips

1 baguette (omit for wheat- and gluten-free option)

2 pieces fresh chilli, deseeded

**1** Heat 1 tbsp of the vegetable oil in a large frying pan over a high heat, add the mushrooms and fry for a few minutes until golden. Add the palm sugar and yellow curry paste, reduce the heat to medium and cook for 3–4 minutes. Add the chilli paste, coconut milk and roasted peanuts and mix well for 2 minutes. Season with salt and pepper and transfer to a bowl.

**2** Top with the spring onions and serve warm with bread, if you like, and fresh chilli on the side.

# Tempeh skewers
## in a sweet soy marinade

Often sold in Indonesia as a street-food snack, these are a great addition to a vegan barbecue – and they also work well as a starter or even a main course if served with rice and greens. The salty, sweet and sour marinade works brilliantly to add depth to the tempeh, and once you've discovered the star ingredient of the marinade, kecap manis (Indonesian sweet soy sauce), it's sure to become one of your favourite condiments. Available from Asian grocers, it's thick and almost treacle-like and absolutely delicious added to stir-fries and rice dishes.

200g/7oz/⅔ block tempeh, cut into cubes

a handful of Crispy Fried Shallots (green onions) (p.48) or crispy fried Thai shallots (p.74)

**For the marinade**
1½ tbsp olive oil
1 large garlic clove, sliced
1 tsp coriander seeds
a pinch of ground cumin
3 tbsp kecap manis
a handful of chopped fresh coriander (cilantro)

**For the dipping sauce**
4 tbsp kecap manis
4 shallots (green onions), finely sliced
1–2 red chillies, deseeded and sliced
juice of ½ lime

**1** Put the tempeh cubes in a steamer and steam for 10 minutes.

**2** Meanwhile, make the marinade. Heat ½ tbsp of the olive oil over a high heat and fry the garlic slices for a few minutes until golden, then remove them from the pan. Toast the coriander seeds in a dry pan until fragrant, then grind them with the cumin using a pestle and mortar. Add the garlic slices, remaining olive oil, kecap manis and fresh coriander and mix thoroughly.

**3** When the tempeh is ready, add it to the marinade, making sure the cubes are completely coated. Leave to marinate at room temperature for at least 1 hour.

**4** Prepare the dipping sauce by simply combining all the ingredients in a bowl.

**5** When you're ready to eat, put the tempeh on metal or soaked wooden skewers and grill (broil) on medium for about 10 minutes, turning halfway through until golden. Serve sprinkled with Crispy Fried Shallots, and with the dipping sauce on the side or poured over the top.

# Vietnamese summer rolls

MAKES
10–15 ROLLS
WF | GF

These light, super-fresh rolls are a great healthy alternative to the more common deep-fried spring roll. A heady mix of crispy vegetables, supple leaves, fragrant herbs and thin chewy noodles, the name of the game here is to simply fill your rice paper sheets with as much raw good stuff as you can. Here's our preferred take on them, but you can experiment as much as you like with different fillings.

350g/2oz pack rice papers
1 batch Sweet Chilli Dipping Sauce (p.168) to serve
lime wedges to serve

### For the dressing
3 Thai shallots (green onions), roughly chopped
2 garlic cloves, crushed
1 tsp chopped coriander root (buy coriander with its roots still on)
2½ tbsp palm sugar
2 long red chillies, deseeded and roughly chopped
2 tsp tamari (make sure it's gluten free)
2 pinches of salt
100ml/3½fl oz/scant ½ cup lime juice

### For the filling
100g/3½oz rice vermicelli
1 carrot, cut into thin batons
1 cucumber, cut into thin batons
½ mango, cut into thin strips
100g/3½oz/⅔ cup cherry tomatoes, halved
50g/1¾oz/⅓ cup roasted peanuts, crushed
a handful of fresh mint leaves
a handful of Thai basil

**1** Pour some boiling water over the rice vermicelli and leave it until it's rehydrated but not too soggy. This should take about 10 minutes. When it's ready, drain, then refresh by placing it in a bowl of ice-cold water for a couple of minutes. Drain again and set aside.

**2** Meanwhile make the dressing. Using a pestle a mortar, grind the shallots, garlic, coriander root, palm sugar, red chillies, tamari, salt and lime juice until they're well combined. Taste – you're looking for that perfect blend of salt, sweet, sour and spicy, so adjust accordingly if you think it doesn't quite hit the spot.

**3** To make the rolls, pour the dressing over the noodles and leave to marinate for about 15 minutes. Prepare a bowl of cold water big enough to submerge a rice paper in, and set aside a damp cloth.

**4** Take a rice paper, briefly submerge it in the cold water, then place it on the damp cloth for about 15 seconds. You want it to be moist but not too wet as they can tear. Place a little of the marinated noodles slightly off-centre, then top with the carrot, cucumber, mango, tomatoes, peanuts and herbs. Roll once over, then tuck the ends in and continue the roll. It's important not to put too much mixture in each roll – use a bit less than you think you'll need. Repeat until you have used all the ingredients. Serve with the sauce and lime wedges to squeeze over the top.

# Banh mi chay

SERVES 4

A result of French colonialism in Vietnam, this popular sandwich is a deft fusion of traditional French produce and native Vietnamese ingredients. The classic version makes use of various Vietnamese cold cuts, but a vegetarian take on the dish using tofu or seitan is often prepared, particularly at Buddhist temples during special religious events. Here's our vegan version.

### For the pickle

500ml/17fl oz/generous 2 cups warm water
100g/3½oz/½ cup brown sugar
100ml/3½fl oz/scant ½ cup rice wine vinegar (brown rice if possible)
2 tbsp salt
150g/5½oz/generous 1 cup carrots, grated
150g/5½oz/1 cup daikon (aka mooli or white radish), grated

### For the miso tofu

60ml/2fl oz/¼ cup sake or white wine
60ml/2fl oz/¼ cup mirin
3 tbsp brown sugar
4 tbsp white miso paste (sometimes known as sweet miso)
oil for greasing
400g/14oz/1¼ blocks firm tofu, cut into 12 slices

### For the rest

4 single-serving baguettes or 2 large baguettes, halved
4 tbsp vegan mayonnaise
1 cucumber, cut into long thin strips
½ bunch of fresh coriander (cilantro), leaves only

1 Make the pickle by mixing the warm water, sugar, vinegar and salt until everything is dissolved. Mix together the carrots and daikon and place in a sterilized, sealable jar. Add the liquid and seal. Leave for an hour to infuse. (You can also make it in advance and it will keep for 2–3 days in the fridge).

2 While it's infusing, preheat the oven to 180°C/350°F/gas mark 4. Next put the sake, mirin and sugar in a pan and bring to the boil, stirring occasionally. Whisk in the miso paste and return to the boil, stirring continuously. Remove from the heat as soon as it reaches boiling point, then leave to cool. (Once cool, this can live in the fridge for up to 2 weeks, so it's another thing that can easily be made in advance.)

3 Put a lightly oiled sheet of greaseproof (waxed) paper on a baking tray, then add the tofu slices. Using half the miso mixture, coat each slice and place in the oven for about 15 minutes until they start to caramelize. Turn them over, coat with the remaining miso and place in the oven for a further 15 minutes. Remove and place to one side.

4 Cut open the baguettes and begin by spreading 1 tbsp mayonnaise on each one. Then simply layer the sandwiches with the tofu, pickle, cucumber and coriander. Top with the other half of the bread and enjoy!

# Courgette primavera

Courgette ribbons serve as linguine in our take on this classic Italian dish. Primavera means spring, and this is a light, herby, colourful dish that showcases the best of the season's vegetable harvest. You can experiment with seasonal vegetables or use whatever takes your fancy. A spiralizer is the easiest way to create authentic-looking linguine, but you can use a potato peeler to shave thin strips of courgette, then cut them into ribbons.

4 courgettes (zucchini), cut into linguine-esque ribbons

1 bunch of asparagus, shaved into strips with a potato peeler

225g/8oz/2½ cups button mushrooms, thinly sliced

½ red onion, finely sliced

1 red (bell) pepper, deseeded and thinly sliced

100g/3½oz/1⅔ cups sun-dried tomatoes, thinly sliced

80g/3oz/scant ½ cup black olives, pitted and thinly sliced

**For the sauce**

1 bunch of fresh basil, plus extra to garnish

½ bunch of fresh parsley, plus extra to garnish

60g/2¼oz/½ cup pine nuts

75ml/2½fl oz/generous ¼ cup olive oil

1 garlic clove

2 tbsp nutritional yeast

salt and pepper

**1** First make the sauce by putting all the ingredients in a blender and combining until smooth.

**2** Mix all the other ingredients in a bowl , pour over the sauce and toss together gently. Garnish with extra basil and parsley and serve.

# Bhel puri

An Indian street-food classic usually served in a cone made from yesterday's newspaper, bhel puri is a riotous explosion of flavours and textures. Typifying the Gujurati art of perfectly balancing sweet, salty, sour and spicy, as well as artfully combining textures, with the crispness of puffed rice and sev perfectly placed against the softness of the boiled potatoes and tomatoes, it's easy to understand why bhel puri enjoys an almost iconic status in parts of India. Prepare all the components in advance, but don't combine them until you're ready to enjoy it, otherwise it's likely to go a bit soggy. Check out Horn OK Please or the Everybody Lovelove Jhal Muri Express – brilliant street-food traders who specialize in this wonderful dish! All the ingredients are readily available from large supermarkets or an Indian grocery. However, if you're struggling to find sev (long fried strands of gram flour) or papdis (fried flour wafers), we sometimes use the equivalent amount of Bombay mix as a substitute. The chutney recipe makes a generous amount, so you can keep it in an airtight jar in the fridge for at least a month, so it will save time when making the next batch.

### For the tamarind chutney

500ml/17floz/generous 2 cups water

50g/1¾oz tamarind paste

100g/3½oz medjool dates, pitted

100g/3½oz/⅓ cup molasses

1 long red chilli, deseeded and chopped

½ tsp ground cumin, lightly roasted in a dry pan

1 thin slice fresh root ginger

½ tsp chat masala

### For the rest

350g/12oz/3½ cups puffed rice, (Rice Krispies work well), toasted in a dry pan until slightly golden

5 new potatoes, boiled and cut into small cubes

100g/3½oz/1 cup mung beans, boiled

2 plum tomatoes, finely diced

2 shallots (green onions), finely chopped

3 tbsp roasted peanuts, lightly crushed

a handful of fresh coriander (cilantro), chopped

1 tbsp lemon juice

1 tsp ground cumin, lightly toasted in a dry pan

1 tsp chat masala

a pinch of chilli powder

a handful of sev

5–6 papdis, broken into pieces (omit for wheat- and gluten-free option)

salt and pepper

**1** To make the chutney, heat the water in a pan over a medium-high heat. Remove any seeds and fibre from the tamarind and dates. When the water has reached the boil, add all the chutney ingredients and let it return to the boil, then simmer for about 10 minutes. Leave to cool for a couple of hours.

**2** Transfer the mixture to a blender and blitz until smooth. Pour the mixture back into the pan and return to the boil. Leave to cool again, then transfer to a sterilized jar or bottle for storage.

**3** Mix all the other ingredients together in a bowl and stir in about 3 tbsp of the chutney. Serve immediately – we love to serve this in newspaper cones for quirky presentation.

**SERVES 4**

# Vegetable tempura
## with a citrus soy dipping sauce

Tempura is a popular Japanese dish of battered and deep-fried seafood or vegetables. It's surprisingly easy to make at home and makes a very enjoyable starter, or it can also be served over soba (buckwheat) noodles as more of a main meal. Interestingly the dish didn't actually originate in Japan, but was introduced there during the 16th century by the Portuguese – a very early example of fusion food! Best served hot.

90g/3¼ oz/¾ cup plain (all-purpose) flour, plus a little extra to dust

1 heaped tsp cornflour (cornstarch)

½ tsp salt

200ml/7fl oz/scant cup ice-cold sparkling water with a few ice cubes

sunflower or vegetable oil to deep-fry

100g/3½oz/1 cup aubergine (eggplant), cut into rounds about 0.5cm/¼in thick

100g/3½oz/scant 1 cup courgette (zucchini), cut into strips about 0.5cm/¼in thick

100g/3½oz/1¼ cups broccoli, cut into florets

20g/¾oz Japanese shiso leaf (optional)

100g/3½oz/scant ½ cup baby corn

100g/3½oz/⅔ cup sweet potato, cut into rounds about 0.5cm/¼in thick

½ avocado, peeled, stoned and sliced

**For the dipping sauce**

1 tbsp + 1 tsp tamari

2 tsp rice wine vinegar (brown if possible)

1 tbsp brown sugar

a little orange zest

2 tsp orange juice

**1** Preheat the oven to 140°C/275°F/gas mark 1. Line a baking tray with greaseproof (waxed) paper and place it in the oven.

**2** To make the batter, mix the two flours and salt in a bowl and whisk in the sparkling water and ice to make a smooth batter.

**3** Put the oil in a wok and heat to 180–190°C/350–375°F or until a cube of bread browns in 20 seconds. In small batches, dust the vegetables with a little plain flour so that they're lightly coated, then dip into the tempura batter and drop into the hot oil. Have a slotted spoon to hand to remove them after about 2 minutes, or when they begin to turn golden brown. Put into a bowl with some kitchen paper (paper towels) on the bottom to absorb the oil, then put in the oven with the door slightly ajar to keep them nice and crisp while you make the next batch. Monitor the oil to make sure it doesn't get too hot – regulate the heat accordingly.

**4** For the dipping sauce, simply combine all the ingredients in a bowl, then serve with the crispy tempura.

# Sweet potato, quinoa and lime corn tortillas with refried beans

Corn tortillas are a delicious staple of the Mexican diet and are a great option for an easy lunch or simple dinner for those avoiding wheat and gluten. We love using quinoa whenever we can and it makes a great filling for these tortillas. Easy to cook and extremely tasty, quinoa is a true superfood. Even NASA declared it to be the ideal snack for astronauts on long-term missions, because it's loaded with protein, minerals and essential amino acids – and it's gluten-free to boot. This recipe makes about 16 small tortillas, which should serve 4 – but not if you're inviting Dave, who can manage 8 on his own!

3 sweet potatoes, cut into thin wedges

1 tbsp olive oil

200g/7 oz/1 cup quinoa

12 cherry tomatoes, chopped

4 shallots (green onions), finely chopped

2 garlic cloves, chopped

1 chilli, deseeded and chopped

½ spring onion (scallion), chopped

2 handfuls of fresh coriander (cilantro), plus extra to garnish

juice of 1 lime, plus extra wedges to serve

16 small round corn tortillas (make sure you get pure corn tortillas)

salt

**For the refried black beans**

1 onion, finely chopped

2 tsp olive oil

1 garlic clove, chopped

½ chipotle chilli, soaked and chopped

½ tsp ground cumin

a pinch of ground cinnamon

400g/14oz tinned black beans, drained and rinsed

**1** Preheat the oven to 200°C/400°F/gas mark 6. Mix the sweet potatoes in a bowl with the olive oil and a little salt, then place on a baking tray and roast for about 25–30 minutes, or until nice and golden.

**2** At the same time, put the quinoa in a pan with double its volume of water and a pinch of salt. Bring to the boil, then simmer for about 20 minutes until tender. Drain and set aside.

**3** While the quinoa is cooking, put the tomatoes, shallots, garlic, chilli, spring onion, coriander and lime juice in a bowl and mix thoroughly. Add the quinoa when it's cooked.

**4** To make the refried beans, sauté the onion in the olive oil for a couple of minutes until translucent. Add the garlic, chipotle, cumin and cinnamon and sauté for a further couple of minutes, then add the black beans. Continue to cook for about 10 minutes, crushing them as they cook with a potato masher.

**5** Lightly warm the tortillas by placing them individually in a dry hot frying pan for about 20 seconds on each side. Lay them flat, smear with a little of the black bean mixture, then add a layer of the quinoa mixture and some sweet potato wedges. Fold over, garnish with coriander and serve with lime wedges for squeezing over.

SALADS

# Som tam salad

SERVES 2
WF | GF
RAW

Som tam is a spicy, green-papaya salad eaten under various guises throughout South East Asia, either as a snack or with sticky rice or noodles. When you order one of these on the street, it is standard practice for the customer to tell the vendor exactly how he or she wants it done. As with so much of Asian cuisine, it really uses the five tastes: sour (lime), bitter (green papaya), sweet (palm sugar), hot (red chilli) and salty (er, salt). The key lies in combining these tastes to best effect, but it is a matter of personal preference, so don't be afraid to experiment. A big pestle and mortar are vital for this recipe – the name translates as 'sour pounded' – as manual grinding really releases the flavours in the dish.

1 small green papaya

1 long red chilli (or bird's-eye if you can take the heat!)

1 large garlic clove

1 tbsp + 1 tsp palm sugar

70g/2½oz/½ cup dry-roasted peanuts

40g/1½oz/scant ½ cup green beans, cut into 2.5cm/1in sticks

6 cherry tomatoes, halved

3 generous pinches of salt , plus extra to taste

1 tbsp + 2 tsp lime juice

½ mango, peeled, stoned and thinly sliced

4 sprigs fresh coriander (cilantro), leaves only

**1** Prepare the green papaya by first peeling it, then using the peeler to shave strips off. Then take your knife and finely slice the strips before leaving to one side.

**2** Pound the chilli and garlic using a pestle and mortar until they form a paste. Add the palm sugar and continue pounding until the sugar is completely dissolved, then add the peanuts and pound until they're crushed. Add the green beans and pound them until they're crushed as well. Add the cherry tomatoes and pound them, too, until all their juice is released. Next add the green papaya strips and just keep on pounding (this recipe is very good for releasing pent-up emotions). If you find that it doesn't all fit in your pestle and mortar, just put half the mixture to one side and pound it in batches.

**3** Add the salt and lime juice and keep on going to combine it all. Serve in a bowl and garnish with mango slivers and coriander leaves.

# Chard rolls with daikon dressing

These raw rolls are so quick and easy to throw together and are laden with nutritional benefits. Swiss chard is another of the wonder greens: it's loaded with antioxidants, omega-3 fatty acids and a huge number of other vitamins, minerals and phytonutrients. It's also absolutely delicious and a true joy to behold, especially in its rainbow variety if you're able to get hold of it. Note that the dressing really must be used on the same day it's made.

**For the Daikon Dressing**

40g/1½oz fresh root ginger, peeled and sliced

1 large shallot (green onion)

75g/2¾oz daikon (aka mooli or white radish), roughly chopped

100ml/3½fl oz/scant ½ cup rice vinegar (brown if possible)

1 tbsp + 2 tsp tamari (make sure it's gluten free)

125ml/4fl oz/½ cup cold-pressed grapeseed oil

1 garlic clove, roughly chopped

**For the rest**

4 chard leaves (Swiss or rainbow)

100g/3½oz mixed sprouts, homemade (p.166) or store-bought

100g/3½oz/¾ cup daikon, thinly sliced

½ cucumber, cut into thin strips

1 red (bell) pepper, deseeded and cut into thin strips

a handful of pea shoots

1 avocado, peeled, stoned and cut into thin strips

2 tsp white sesame seeds

1 apple, cored and thinly sliced

a handful of fresh flat-leaf parsley

**1** Make the dressing by simply placing everything in a blender and combining until smooth. Set aside.

**2** Place each chard leaf down flat on a board. With a paring knife, cut out the thickest part of each stem to leave two points. Put one point over the other, then place a generous mixture of all the vegetables in the middle and roll it up, leaving one end exposed.

**3** Serve with a ramekin of the dressing for dipping.

SERVES 4
WF | GF | RAW

# Kale and avocado salad

Kale really seems to be in vogue at the moment and what a great thing that is. It tastes great and it's a real nutritional powerhouse. Kale is packed with antioxidants, iron, fibre, calcium, vitamins A, C and K; it helps lower cholesterol levels, detoxifies the body and so the list goes on. This is such an easy-to-make salad and it's a great way of getting more raw food into your diet. The process of massaging the kale with the oil, lemon and salt breaks down its tough cellulose structure, changing it from a slightly bitter, hardy leaf into a kind of soft and sweet state that's great for salads and much easier to enjoy. You'll see the kale transform as you massage (it likes the deep-tissue technique, so be firm!); the leaves will darken and shrink and become silky-smooth.

400g/14oz/5¾ cups kale, stalks removed, leaves chopped

½ red onion, finely chopped

1 garlic clove, finely chopped

juice of 1 lemon

2 tbsp + 2 tsp olive oil

a pinch of cayenne pepper

1 tsp nutritional yeast (make sure it's gluten free)

2 avocados, peeled, stoned and cut into large pieces

salt and pepper

**1** Put everything except the avocado in a large bowl, season with salt and pepper and massage thoroughly with your fingertips.

**2** When the kale appears slightly wilted and everything is well combined, transfer to a serving plate, top with the avocado pieces and serve.

# Hot aubergine salad

SERVES 4
WF | GF

This unusual way of preparing aubergines (eggplant) works well as a simple meal served with brown rice. However, with its Chinese flavours, it also makes a great accompaniment to any Asian-inspired meal. For best results, serve it straight from the wok.

2 aubergines (eggplant), cut into 2.5cm/1in rounds

vegetable oil, for frying

salt

### For the dressing

1 tbsp vegetable oil

1 red chilli, deseeded and sliced

30g/1oz fresh root ginger, peeled and thinly sliced

4 garlic cloves, puréed

1 tbsp + 2 tsp tamari  (make sure it's gluten free)

200ml/7fl oz/scant 1 cup Shaoxing rice wine (or white wine if unavailable)

50g/1¾oz/¼ cup brown sugar

2 tbsp rice wine vinegar (brown if possible)

4 spring onions (scallions), thinly sliced

a handful of fresh coriander (cilantro) leaves

**1** Sprinkle the aubergine slices with salt, then leave to stand for 2 hours. Rinse off the salt and dry the aubergine with kitchen paper (paper towels). Working in batches, pour a little oil in a frying pan and add the aubergine slices, frying until the pieces are half-cooked and just beginning to soften and adding more oil to the pan as necessary. Remove from the pan and drain well on kitchen paper.

**2** To make the dressing, heat the oil in a wok and fry the chilli, ginger and garlic for 2 minutes until they begin to soften. Next, add the tamari and Shaoxing wine and cook until the alcohol has burned off. Add the sugar and stir until dissolved, then add the rice vinegar.

**3** To finish the dish, add three-quarters of the spring onions to the dressing in the wok, heat to boiling point, then add 5–6 slices of aubergine and cook in the dressing for about 4 minutes until tender. Repeat until you've used up all your aubergine, keeping the cooked slices warm. Garnish with the remaining spring onion slices and the coriander and serve immediately.

SERVES 2
WF | GF | RAW

# Oyster mushroom and avocado ceviche salad

Ceviche is a dish popular throughout coastal regions of the Americas, in particular in Peru, where a national holiday is even held in its honour. Typically made with fresh raw fish, ceviche actually refers to the technique whereby the fish (or in this case, oyster mushroom) is marinated in citrus juices – usually lemon or lime. Not only does this add a lovely flavour, but the citric acid also denatures the proteins in the dish, giving it the appearance and texture of being 'cooked'. This makes it a fantastic process for raw food!

150g/5½oz/1½ cups oyster mushrooms, torn

100ml/3½fl oz/scant ½ cup lime juice

1 tbsp finely chopped red onion

2 tbsp extra virgin olive oil

1 tbsp coconut palm nectar or agave syrup

2 handfuls of chopped fresh coriander (cilantro)

1 spring onion (scallion), thinly sliced

15g/½oz dulse seaweed, shredded

½ red chilli, deseeded and sliced

1 avocado

2 baby gem or other salad leaves

salt and pepper

**1** Mix the mushrooms, lime juice and onion in a bowl. Cover with clingfilm (plastic wrap) and chill in the fridge for about 2 hours.

**2** Remove from the fridge and squeeze off the excess lime juice into a small bowl. Mix in the olive oil and palm nectar, then season with salt and pepper and place to one side.

**3** Add the coriander, spring onion, dulse, chilli and a little more salt to the mushrooms, then peel, stone and slice the avocado.

**4** On a bed of salad leaves, add the avocado and ceviche mushrooms. Dress to taste with the olive oil and lime mixture and serve.

# Caesar salad

Hailed by many as the 'King of Salads', this vegan take on a much-loved dish is not traditional but it certainly honours the spirit of the original. Garlicky and slightly cheesy thanks to the nutritional yeast and 'raw' mesan, once you've had this you'll find it's something you'll really start to crave. The dulse also works brilliantly in place of anchovies or Worcestershire sauce to add a slightly seafood-like taste. Assemble at the table for dramatic flair as they did at Caesar Cardini's Tijuana restaurant, where it's said this dish originated. If you like the raw mesan, it makes a great topping for many other dishes, too, such as Courgette Primavera (p.57) or Raw 'Lasagne' (p.110).

**For the dressing**
2 tbsp lemon juice
2 tbsp nutritional yeast
1 garlic clove
1 tsp tamari (make sure it's gluten free)
1 tbsp Dijon mustard
80ml/3fl oz/⅓ cup olive oil
130g/4½oz/scant 1 cup cashews

**For the croûtons (omit for wheat- and gluten-free diets)**
5 slices sourdough bread, cut into cubes
80ml/3fl oz/⅓ cup olive oil

**For the raw mesan**
60g/2¼oz/scant ½ cup pine nuts
2 tbsp nutritional yeast (make sure it's gluten free)
salt and pepper

**For the salad**
1 head romaine lettuce, chopped
15g/½oz dulse seaweed, shredded

**1** Make the dressing by combining all the ingredients in a blender or food processor, adjusting the seasoning to taste. If possible, leave for about an hour before using to infuse the flavours.

**2** Meanwhile, make the croûtons. Preheat the oven to 180°C/350°F/gas mark 4. Mix the bread cubes with the olive oil in a bowl and season with salt and pepper. Transfer to a baking sheet, then bake for about 10 minutes, moving them around every couple of minutes, until golden and crispy.

**3** Next, make your 'raw' mesan by putting all the ingredients in a blender and combining until the mixture resembles a fine powder.

**4** Finally, assemble the salad by mixing the romaine lettuce and dulse with the salad dressing and the croûtons. Sprinkle the 'raw' mesan over the top and you're ready to go!

# Quinoa salad

## with green mustard dressing

Quinoa (keen-wah) is actually a seed, not a grain, but in any case it's a brilliant alternative to rice or couscous and is something we serve a lot at home. It's considered a superfood, as it's a complete protein and contains eight essential amino acids as well as having numerous other benefits. It might seem light and fluffy but it really fills you up without bogging you down and makes a fantastic base for this zesty salad. A spiralizer is a really good piece of equipment for making vegetable ribbons that look beautiful in salads. It's well worth investing in one, but just use a grater if you don't have one to hand.

**For the salad**

360g/12⅔oz/1½ cups quinoa

1 litre/34fl oz/1 quart water

2 carrots, grated

2 oranges, peeled, segmented, then cut in half

zest of ¼ orange

80g/2¾oz/⅔ cup flaked almonds, toasted

60g/2¾oz/½ cup raisins

2 handfuls of fresh parsley leaves

2 spring onions (scallions), finely sliced

a handful of mixed sprouts, homemade (p.166) or store-bought

2 beetroot, peeled and spiralized or grated, to garnish

salt and pepper

**For the Green Mustard Dressing**

100ml/3½fl oz/scant ½ cup olive oil

1 tbsp + 2 tsp apple cider vinegar

1 tbsp Dijon mustard

1 tsp agave syrup or other sweetener

a handful of fresh parsley

a handful of fresh basil

**1** Rinse the quinoa for a minute or so, then drain. Bring the water to the boil in a pan, then add the quinoa and a couple of pinches of salt. Cook on a medium heat for 10–12 minutes until the water is absorbed. Put in a strainer to drain any traces of water before spreading it out on a tray to cool.

**2** While the quinoa cools, make the dressing by putting all the ingredients in a blender and combining until smooth. Season with salt and pepper to taste.

**3** Assemble the salad by gently mixing the quinoa with the dressing and all the salad ingredients, except the beetroot. Garnish with the beetroot and serve.

# Aromatic thai salad

Served in individual lettuce cups, this salad is great as a canapé or for sharing, and the flavours immediately transport you to the Far East. The miang kham sauce lasts a couple of weeks in the fridge, so it can be made in advance and any leftovers can be saved for future use. Supermarkets are increasingly stocking most of the unusual ingredients used here, and they will all be readily available from Asian grocers. We always stock up on lots of galangal, lemongrass and kaffir lime leaves when we go, and put them in the freezer so we don't always have to make a special trip. Crispy fried Thai shallots are available prepared in Asian stores, or you can use our Crispy Fried Shallots (p.48).

**For the miang kham**

4 kaffir lime leaves

2 sticks lemongrass

1 red chilli

3 Thai shallots (or normal small ones if Thai are unavailable)

1 garlic clove

40g/1½oz galangal, peeled

200g/7oz/1 cup palm sugar

200ml/7fl oz/scant 1 cup water

60g/2¼oz/⅔ cup desiccated coconut

2 tbsp soy sauce

**For the salad**

1 bunch of spring onions (scallions), cut into thin strips

3 Thai shallots (or normal ones, if unavailable), finely sliced

20g/¾oz crispy fried Thai shallots or Crispy Fried Shallots (p.48) (optional)

50g/1¾oz/⅓ cup crushed roasted peanuts

1 pomelo or white grapefruit

1 pomegranate, seeded

½ bunch of fresh coriander (cilantro), chopped

½ bunch of fresh mint, chopped

½ red chilli, deseeded and thinly sliced

zest and juice of 1 lime

2 heads of baby gem or chicory leaves

**1** First make the miang kham. Crush all the dry ingredients except the sugar and coconut using a pestle and mortar. In a pan, melt the palm sugar with the water.

**2** Add all the crushed ingredients, bring to the boil, then reduce the heat and simmer for 15–20 minutes until the mixture slightly thickens. Remove from the heat and leave to cool.

**3** Meanwhile, toast the coconut in a dry frying pan over a medium heat, stirring continuously, for approximately 2–3 minutes, or until lightly golden. Quickly remove from the hot pan and set aside.

**4** Once the sauce has cooled, pour it through a sieve, then add the toasted coconut and soy sauce. Set aside while you prepare the salad.

**5** Mix all the salad ingredients except the lime zest and juice and the baby gem, in a large bowl. Mix in about 3 tbsp of the miang kham, then add the lime zest and juice and stir.

**6** Pull the leaves from the baby gem to make individual serving cups, or simply arrange them on a plate, then put a little of the mixture into each one and serve.

# Raw bowl

SERVES 4
WF | GF | RAW

This is for those times when you feel in a need of a real boost, offering your 5-a-day and then some! If you have a dehydrator, soak the seeds for 8 hours, drain, then place on a Teflex sheet in the dehydrator set to 45°C/113°F for 24 hours; if not, just use the seeds raw. Feel free to make any substitutions – as long as it's nutritious, put it in!

**For the cauliflower rice**

1 cauliflower, roughly chopped

a handful of pine nuts

a pinch of salt

a dash of apple cider vinegar

1 bunch of fresh chives, finely chopped

a dash of sesame oil

**For the marinated mushrooms**

200g/7oz/2¼ cups oyster mushrooms, shredded

1½ tbsp tamari (make sure it's gluten free)

1 garlic clove, chopped

1 tbsp palm sugar nectar or agave syrup

1 spring onion (scallion), green part only, finely chopped

juice of ½ lemon

**For the rest**

4 handfuls of mixed salad leaves

2 avocados, peeled, stoned and sliced

100g/3½oz/1 cup Kimchi (p.146) or Sauerkraut (p.148)

1 batch Sunomono (p.117)

1 batch Raw Sesame Dressing (p.167)

200g/7oz/2 cups mixed sprouts, homemade (p.166) or store-bought

100g/3½oz/⅔ cup mixed seeds (sesame, sunflower, flaxseed, poppy, chia)

2 limes, halved

**1** Mix all the ingredients for the mushrooms together in a bowl. Cover and leave to marinate in the fridge for 1 hour.

**2** Roughly process the cauliflower in a food processor or blender until it begins to resemble rice grains. Add the pine nuts at the last minute and pulse once or twice more. Place the mixture in a bowl and season with the salt, cider vinegar, chives and sesame oil.

**3** Put the cauliflower rice in the middle of each of four serving bowls. Surround with salad leaves, then build up using all the other ingredients, leaving the sprouts, seeds and dressing until last. Serve the bowls with lime halves for squeezing over.

# Chopped salad

You'll need a sharp knife for this, because in case you hadn't guessed from the name, the essence of this salad is freshly chopped ingredients. It's a great chance to hone your chopping skills but it's also an incredibly straightforward super-salad. The world's your oyster in terms of ingredients, we've suggested our favourite combination but you can use whatever you have to hand to make it – try out any ingredients that catch your eye. This dressing is delicious, but make sure you use it fresh as it doesn't keep well.

**1** Mix together all the ingredients for the dressing except the oil. When well combined, whisk in the oil until it's fully incorporated. Season to taste.

**2** Mix all the salad ingredients together. Pour the dressing over the top and enjoy!

### For the dressing

50g/1¾oz Thai shallots, or other small shallots (green onions), finely sliced

1 garlic clove, finely chopped

1 tbsp + 2 tsp tamari (make sure it's gluten free)

30g/1oz tahini

2 tbsp rice wine vinegar (brown if possible)

1 tbsp orange juice

¼ tsp wasabi paste (make sure it's gluten free)

100ml/3½fl oz/scant ½ cup grapeseed oil or extra light olive oil

salt and pepper

### For the salad

350g/12oz/1 block smoked tofu, sliced

½ iceberg lettuce, chopped

1 radicchio, chopped

1 romaine lettuce heart, chopped

100g/3½oz watercress, picked

2–3 spring onions (scallions), chopped

½ cucumber, chopped

100g/3½oz/¾ cup mixed seeds (flaxseed, sunflower, poppy, sesame), lightly toasted

80g/3oz/½ cup walnuts, lightly toasted

250g/9oz cherry tomatoes

100g/3½oz mixed sprouts, homemade (p.166) or store-bought

1 red (bell) pepper, deseeded and chopped

10 radishes, chopped

a handful of fresh parsley, chopped

2 celery sticks, chopped

# < Raw sprouted salad

SERVES 4
WF | GF | RAW

This is a fresh, crisp and nutritious salad that makes a fantastic lunch. It's so colourful and vibrant that it makes you feel better just by looking at it! It tastes great served with raw crackers and spreads.

100g/3½oz/⅔ cup cherry tomatoes, halved • 200g/7oz mixed sprouts (mung beans, lentils, alfalfa), homemade (p.166) or store-bought • a handful of fresh flat-leaf parsley • 100g/3½oz/2 cups baby spinach • 100g/3½oz/heaped ¾ cup walnuts • 1 red (bell) pepper, deseeded and chopped • 150g/5½oz/1½ cups red cabbage, thinly shredded • 2 carrots, grated • 2 dessert apples, cored and thinly sliced • 100g/3½oz/1 cup celery, chopped • 100g/3½oz/¾ cup radish, chopped • 100g/3½oz/scant 1½ cups beetroot, spiralized if possible but otherwise grated • 1 batch Basic Raw Salad Dressing (p.166)

Simply combine all the ingredients in a large bowl, dress and serve.

# Asian slaw

SERVES 4
WF | GF | RAW

This is a really simple salad dish that goes well with many main courses, especially 'Pulled' Jackfruit Sliders (p.105).

¼ white cabbage, finely sliced • ¼ red cabbage, finely sliced • ½ white onion, finely sliced • 2 carrots, grated • 2 spring onions (scallions), thinly sliced • 2–3 tbsp mixed seeds • 1 small bunch of fresh mint, roughly chopped • 5 tbsp rice wine vinegar (brown if possible) • 3 tbsp agave nectar • 1 tsp sesame oil

**1** Put the vegetables, seeds and the mint in a bowl and mix to combine.

**2** Whisk together the rice vinegar, agave nectar and sesame oil in another bowl. Pour the dressing over the vegetables, toss well and serve.

CURRIES
& MAINS

# Beer-battered tofu 'fish' and chips

## with tartare sauce and mushy peas

Oh, this is a lovely treat! We're suckers for anything battered once in a while and this really hits the spot. The tofu is a wonderful substitute in this classic British dish and the nori really adds the taste of the sea. Served with chunky chips, piquant tartare sauce to liven it up and a healthy dose of mushy peas, this is a dish to treasure. Serve, of course, with cheap malt vinegar.

180g/6oz/1½ cups plain (all-purpose) flour

1 tsp cornflour (cornstarch), plus extra to dust

1½ tsp onion powder

½ tsp garlic powder

1 tsp chilli powder

325ml/11fl oz/1⅓ cups) pale ale
(make sure you get a vegan one)

350g/12oz/1 block fresh firm tofu, drained
and cut into 8–10 slices

1 sheet nori, cut into 8–10 pieces to neatly
put on top of each slice of tofu
salt and pepper

1 lemon, cut into wedges to serve

1 batch Tartare Sauce (p.169) to serve

### For the chips

4–5 King Edward potatoes, peeled,
cut into chunky chip shapes and
left to dry out on a tea towel

750ml/26fl oz/3¼ cups vegetable oil

### For the mushy peas

200g/7oz/1¼ cups fresh or frozen peas

1 tbsp apple cider vinegar

a handful of fresh mint, finely chopped

**1** To make the chips, heat the oil to about 160°C/320°F. When a cube of bread browns in about 40 seconds, put half the chips in – you're going to cook them in two batches – and fry for about 10 minutes until the insides are soft. Keep the temperature constant. Remove with a slotted spoon and leave to drain on a baking sheet covered with kitchen paper (paper towels).

**2** While the chips are draining, make the beer batter by combining the flour, cornflour, onion, garlic and chilli powders with the ale, mixing thoroughly. In a pan, heat the oil to 170°C/340°F. Check the temperature by putting a couple of drops of batter in the oil and seeing if it crisps up.

**3** Dust the tofu and nori slices with a little cornflour, then coat with the batter mixture and add to the hot oil in batches. They should take about 3–4 minutes to get really crisp. Flip them over midway so that they get nice and golden on both sides. Remove with a slotted spoon, place on some kitchen paper to soak up any excess oil and season to taste.

**4** When you're ready to eat, heat the oil to 190°C/375°F, put the chips back in and cook until they're golden and crispy. This should take about 6 minutes. Meanwhile, put the peas in boiling water with a little salt, bring to the boil, then cook for a couple of minutes until they're slightly overdone. Strain, put them back in the pan, then crush with a potato masher, adding a little water if necessary to make them soft. Add the apple cider vinegar and chopped mint. Season with salt and pepper and slowly heat while mixing for a couple of minutes.

**5** Put everything together on a (big!) plate with a generous wedge of lemon and a dollop of Tartare Sauce and enjoy.

# Massaman curry

There are many different ideas as to how and where this dish originated, but one popular theory is that it was born in southern Thailand, where there are many Muslims, hence the name, which means Muslim curry. In any case, it has recently been voted by CNN as the world's most delicious food, and it always draws gasps of 'I love massaman!' when people read it on our menu board.

**For the curry**

1 tbsp tamarind pulp

50ml/2fl oz/3 tbsp hot water

800ml/28fl oz/3⅓ cups coconut milk

1 batch Massaman Curry Paste (p.171)

2 tsp palm sugar

2–3 tbsp tamari, to taste (make sure it's gluten free)

200g/7oz can pineapple chunks in their own juice

80g/3oz/½ cup dry-roasted peanuts

2 sweet potatoes, cut into chunks and roasted

a handful of dried soy chunks (soaked in water for about 30 minutes) or marinated tofu pieces

10 small pickling onions or shallots (green onions), optional

**To finish**

a few leaves of fresh coriander (cilantro)

1 red chilli, deseeded and sliced

a handful of Crispy Fried Shallots (green onions) (p.48) or crispy fried Thai shallots (p.74) (optional)

short-grain brown rice to serve

**1** Soak the tamarind in the hot water for 20 minutes, then pour everything through a sieve into a small bowl, mashing the tamarind through with a spoon.

**2** Put 4 tbsp of the creamiest part of the coconut milk in a dry saucepan over a medium heat. Once it's hot, add the curry paste and cook for 10 minutes on a low heat, stirring occasionally. Add the palm sugar and continue to cook until you see it caramelizing (about 5–10 minutes). By now your house should smell like a Bangkok street market!

**3** Add the rest of the coconut milk and bring to the boil, adding the tamarind water. Simmer for 15 minutes.

**4** Remove from the heat, then pour through a sieve into a bowl to remove any gritty bits. Pour back into the saucepan and add the tamari and 4 tbsp pineapple juice from the can. Return to the heat, bring to the boil again, add the peanuts, sweet potatoes, pineapple chunks, soy chunks and pickling onions and slowly simmer for a further 20 minutes.

**5** Check the seasoning and add a little more tamari if you feel it's needed. Garnish with red chilli, coriander and Crispy Fried Shallots and serve with steamed short-grain brown rice.

# Korma

This sweet, creamy curry is just one of those things you sometimes crave, and although it's often made with yogurt or cream, our mix of cashew nuts and coconut milk give it the same level of comforting creaminess. Snuggle up in front of a movie and serve with chapattis and basmati rice for a real treat. We also love to eat our curries with a chutney or pickle, so try that, too. You could also add a dollop of Coconut Yogurt (p.19).

2 tbsp coconut oil (or cooking oil of your choice)

4 black peppercorns

1 dried red chilli, deseeded and finely chopped

½ tsp chilli powder

2 cinnamon sticks

6 green cardamom pods

1 clove

1 tsp turmeric

1½ tbsp coriander seeds, lightly toasted in a pan and then crushed

2 tbsp chopped fresh coriander (cilantro) leaves, plus extra to garnish

1½ tsp garam masala

1 garlic clove, puréed

1½ large onions, puréed

1cm/½in fresh root ginger, peeled and blended with the onion

1 small cauliflower, cut into small florets

250g/9oz/1 cup pumpkin, diced

100g/3½oz/1 cup green beans

200ml/7fl oz/scant 1 cup coconut milk

150g/5½oz/1 cup cashews, soaked for 2 hours

500ml/17fl oz/generous 2 cups water

40g/1½oz/¼ cup sultanas (golden raisins)

salt

cooked basmati rice to serve

1 lime, cut into wedges, to serve

**1** Heat the coconut oil in a pan with the peppercorns, chilli and chilli powder, cinnamon, cardamom, clove, turmeric, coriander seeds and leaves, garam masala, garlic, onion and ginger and slowly cook on a low heat, mixing it around occasionally, while you prepare the vegetables. You want to cook it until there's no longer the smell of raw onion, which should take about 10 minutes.

**2** Add the vegetables and continue to cook over a low heat.

**3** Meanwhile, in a blender, combine the coconut milk and cashews and add to the vegetable mix, along with the water and the sultanas. Leave to simmer for about 30 minutes, stirring occasionally to prevent it from catching. Season to taste, garnish with coriander leaves and serve with basmati rice and lime wedges for squeezing over.

# Chow fun noodles

This is a stir-fried noodle dish that traditionally uses ho fun, a type of wide Chinese rice noodle that is white in colour with a slippery texture. They're extremely satisfying and you'll find them in most Asian supermarkets. Make sure your ingredients are prepared and ready to go before you start cooking as this is one fast dish! It's a really good test of your wok hei, a method of quick cooking over a very high heat that roughly translates as 'breath of the wok'. David likes to line everything up in the order of use so he can go like lightning once the wok is hot. Resist the urge to turn down the heat at any point, and keep the ingredients moving with a large flat metal spoon.

½ onion, thinly sliced

3 tbsp coconut oil (or cooking oil of your choice)

2 garlic cloves, finely sliced

1 red chilli, deseeded and finely sliced

1 carrot, thinly sliced

1 tbsp brown sugar

1 tbsp + 2 tsp tamari, or more to taste (make sure it's gluten free)

½ head broccoli, cut into small florets

1 head pak choy, quartered

2 spring onions (scallions), cut into batons

250g/9oz ho fun noodles

2 handfuls of bean sprouts

a handful of fresh Thai basil

1 tsp toasted sesame oil

**1** Put a wok on the highest heat you can achieve. When it's really hot, throw the onions in and then pour the coconut oil over them (this should stop the oil from spitting so much). Cook for a minute or so until they show the first signs of browning, then add the garlic and chilli and cook for a further minute. Add the carrot and cook for another minute.

**2** Next add the sugar and tamari and carry on cooking for a minute or so before adding the broccoli, pak choy and spring onions, then add the ho fun noodles – stir them in carefully as ho fun are liable to break. Cook for 2–3 minutes, adding a little water around the sides if need be to prevent the mixture from burning and sticking to the pan. When the noodles are showing signs of becoming transparent, add the bean sprouts and Thai basil and cook for a further 2 minutes. Finish by drizzling over the sesame oil and serve.

# Arancini

SERVES 4

Originally from Sicily, arancini are deep-fried risotto balls coated with breadcrumbs. Arancia is the Italian word for an orange, and the real deal in Sicily are not far off the size, with their golden breadcrumbs they're not a dissimilar colour, either, so it's easy to understand where the name comes from. Here we've made them into more of a main meal, served with a tomato sauce and a generous salad, but they're traditionally a street-food snack, designed for eating on the hoof. In London, look out for the Arancini Brothers, who do a great vegan version from their stalls and cafés.

**For the arancini**

1 tbsp olive oil

1 garlic clove, chopped

1 small onion, finely chopped

200g/7oz/¾ cup arborio rice

150ml/5fl oz/generous 1 cup white wine (make sure it's vegan)

2 litres/68fl oz/2 quarts) hot Vegetable Stock, homemade (p.170) or store-bought

1 tbsp finely chopped fresh rosemary leaves

2 tbsp finely chopped fresh flat-leaf parsley

4 tbsp nutritional yeast

250ml/9fl oz/generous 1 cup Soya Milk, homemade (p.157) or store-bought

6 slices stale bread, made into breadcrumbs

400ml/14fl oz/1⅔ cups vegetable oil

salt and pepper

**For the tomato sauce**

1 tbsp olive oil

1 small onion, finely chopped

2 garlic cloves, chopped

5 sun-dried tomatoes, roughly chopped

5 tomatoes on the vine, roughly chopped

1 tsp sugar

a handful of fresh basil, chopped

**To serve**

200g/7oz mixed salad leaves

1 batch Basic Raw Salad Dressing (p.166) or dressing of your choice

**1** To make the arancini, heat the olive oil in a pan and sauté the garlic and onion until transparent. Add the rice and sauté for a further minute or so until the grains are also transparent. Add the white wine and allow it to cook off before adding a ladle of stock at a time, stirring until it's incorporated before adding another ladle, continuing until the rice is cooked (this should take about 15 minutes). Add the herbs and season with the nutritional yeast, salt and pepper, tasting and adjusting the seasoning if necessary. Leave to cool before transferring to the fridge to chill.

**2** While the mixture chills, make the tomato sauce. Heat the olive oil in a pan and sauté the onions until transparent. Add the garlic and lower the heat before adding the sun-dried and vine tomatoes and the sugar and simmer for 30–40 minutes, stirring occasionally until thick and rich. Stir in the basil and season to taste. Set aside and bring back to temperature when the arancini are ready.

**3** Next, prepare 2 small bowls: one for the milk and one for the breadcrumbs. Mould a heaped tablespoon of the arancini mix into a ball shape, then dunk it in the milk before rolling in the breadcrumbs. Repeat until they are all coated – you should end up with 10–12 risotto balls.

**4** Heat the vegetable oil to 160°C/320°F, when a cube of bread will brown in 40 seconds. Fry the balls in the oil in batches until golden brown. Keep the temperature constant. Remove with a slotted spoon and place on a piece of kitchen paper (paper towels) to absorb any excess oil. Serve on a bed of the tomato sauce with a generous dressed green side salad.

# Thai green curry

This has got a little more kick than the Massaman Curry (p.84). Properly made, it's another potent combination of sour, sweet, salt and heat, offset by the soothing creaminess of the coconut, that will assault your taste buds in the best-possible way. Green chillies lend colour and bite, but you can experiment with the remaining ingredients. Aubergines (eggplant), cherry tomatoes and, wait for it, lychees, are our favourite combination! It's a great idea to stock up on things like galangal, fresh turmeric and kaffir lime leaves and keep them in the freezer so you don't have to make a special grocery trip when you want to pack flavour into your dishes.

1 aubergine (eggplant), cubed

a pinch of salt

2 tbsp olive oil

2 tbsp coconut oil (or cooking oil of your choice)

1 batch Thai Green Curry Paste (p.171)

1 tbsp palm sugar

800ml/28fl oz/3½ cups tinned coconut milk

tamari, to taste (make sure it's gluten free)

200g/7oz/1 cup tinned lychees

100g/3½oz/¾ cup mangetout, sliced at an angle

100g/3½oz/scant ½ cup baby corn, cut in half

250g/9oz/1⅔ cups cherry tomatoes

a handful of fresh coriander (cilantro) leaves, from the roots used in the paste (above), plus extra to garnish

a handful of fresh Thai basil leaves, plus extra to garnish

cooked short-grained brown rice (or rice of your choice) to serve

**1** Preheat the oven to 200°C/400°F/gas mark 6. Put the aubergine cubes on a baking sheet, sprinkle over the salt and drizzle with olive oil. Roast for about 20 minutes.

**2** Heat the coconut oil in a pan and add the curry paste. Sauté on a medium heat for 3–4 minutes, then add the palm sugar and let it caramelize. Add the coconut milk and bring it to the boil. Add the tamari to taste and simmer for 15 minutes. At this point you can put the mixture through a strainer to remove any woody bits from the paste.

**3** Return the mix to the pan, bring back to the boil, then add all the fruit and vegetables except the cherry tomatoes. Bring back to the boil and simmer for 2–3 minutes before adding the tomatoes and herbs. Remove from the heat, garnish with extra coriander and Thai basil leaves and serve with brown rice.

# Larb

We first tried this salad, the national dish of Laos, in a tiny place called Pak Beng, the overnight stop for the longboats on the Mekong River when travelling from northern Thailand to Luang Prabang. We didn't have high hopes of getting a good meal that night, so what a lovely surprise when a first-class tofu larb arrived at the table. We went on to try many during our time in Laos and accumulated tips on how to make it as we went. It's great served in iceburg lettuce cups and is good on its own or as a starter or canapé. We also love following the Asian tradition of having meals made up of lots of different dishes, and find larb works really well in that context, too. Traditionally larb is eaten as part of a set alongside Som Tam Salad (p.64) and a bowl of sticky rice.

50g/1¾oz/¼ cup jasmine rice

1½ tbsp coconut oil (or cooking oil of your choice)

3 garlic cloves, puréed

2–3 red chillies, deseeded and very thinly sliced

a pinch of white pepper

1 spring onion (scallion), finely sliced

1½ tsp palm sugar

600g/1lb 5oz/1¾ blocks fresh firm tofu, crumbled and placed on kitchen paper (paper towels) to dry

1 tbsp tamari (make sure it's gluten free)

25g/1oz fresh coriander (cilantro), chopped

a handful of fresh mint, chopped

a handful of fresh Thai basil, chopped

juice of 1 lime

a pinch of salt

1 iceburg lettuce, leaves separated

**1** In a dry wok, toast the dry rice for about 3–5 minutes, until it turns golden, then pour out onto kitchen paper (paper towels) and leave to cool. Once it's cool enough to handle, use a pestle and mortar to crush it well. Set aside.

**2** Heat the wok again before adding the coconut oil, garlic, chillies, white pepper, spring onion, palm sugar and tofu (in that order). Mix well with a spatula to crumble the tofu completely and prevent it from burning while you cook for about 2 minutes. Add the tamari, coriander, mint and basil and continue to cook for a further couple of minutes, stirring constantly. Add the lime juice and a pinch of salt and mix thoroughly.

**3** Spoon into your lettuce cups and top with a sprinkle of the roasted rice to add a nutty crunch.

# Gado-gado

SERVES 4
WF | GF

Gado-gado is a main-dish salad served with peanut sauce and steamed rice that you can find throughout Indonesia. You can buy it from street hawkers, where the dish originated, to five-star hotels. There's great variation in the vegetables used so it's one of those dishes that makes use of whatever you can get hold of – in Indonesian, gado-gado means mix-mix or medley, so feel free to experiment. Imagine you're among the rice paddies of Bali and enjoy.

### For the salad

300g/10½oz/1 block tempeh or fresh firm tofu, drained, cut into bite-size pieces and dusted with cornflour

150–200ml/5–7fl oz/generous ½ cup–scant 1 cup vegetable oil for frying

500g/1lb 2oz/3⅓ cups new potatoes, boiled and quartered

125g/4½oz/scant 1 cup cherry tomatoes, halved

150g/5½oz/1½ cups green beans, blanched

1 iceburg lettuce, cut into pieces

1 cucumber, cut into batons

½ pineapple, cut into long strips

2 limes, halved

2 large handfuls of bean sprouts or mung bean sprouts, homemade (p.166) or store-bought

a handful of fresh coriander (cilantro)

2 long, red chillies, deseeded and sliced

### For the peanut sauce

175g/6oz/scant 1¼ cups peanuts

2 tbsp coconut oil (or oil of your choice)

3 shallots, chopped

2 garlic cloves, chopped

½ long red chilli, chopped

40g/1½oz/3 tbsp palm sugar

400ml/14fl oz/1¾ cups coconut milk

1 tbsp tamari (make sure it's gluten free)

**1** Preheat the oven to 200°C/400°F/gas mark 6. To make the sauce, put the peanuts on a baking sheet and roast for about 5–10 minutes, being careful not to let them burn. Leave to cool, then transfer to a blender and pulse until finely ground.

**2** Next, heat the coconut oil in a saucepan over a medium heat. Add the shallots and sauté for a few minutes until transparent, then add the garlic and chilli and cook for a further 5 minutes.

**3** Sprinkle in the palm sugar, turn the heat down to low and cook until the sugar has completely melted. Pour in the coconut milk and bring to the boil, then leave to simmer for about 10 minutes.

**4** Add the peanuts to the pan and continue to cook until the coconut milk just begins to split. Remove from the heat, season with the tamari and set aside.

**5** Heat the vegetable oil to 180°C/350°F in a large pan and shallow-fry the tempeh or tofu, gently moving the pieces around for 4–5 minutes until lightly browned. Remove from the pan with a slotted spoon and drain on kitchen paper (paper towels).

**6** Assemble all of the remaining salad ingredients on a large serving plate, top with the fried tempeh and serve with the peanut sauce.

# Nasi goreng

SERVES 4

The name translates as 'fried rice' in Indonesian, and nasi goreng is a very satisfying, quick-to-prepare meal. We generally have it as a dinner, though for the brave it is traditionally eaten for breakfast using leftover rice from the previous night – it's Indonesia's bubble and squeak! Fried rice is commonly eaten throughout Asia, but it is the addition of wonder ingredient kecap manis (a sweet soy sauce) that gives nasi goreng its rich, distinctive taste.

2½ tbsp coconut oil (or cooking oil of your choice), for frying

1 batch Nasi Goreng Paste (p.171)

100g/3½oz/scant 1 cup green beans, cut into 2.5cm/1in batons, blanched

1 carrot, finely diced

500g/1lb 2oz/generous 3 cups cooked jasmine rice, cold

4 shallots (green onions), finely chopped

1 tbsp kecap manis

1 tbsp tamari or soy sauce

2 red chillies, deseeded and thinly sliced

a handful of fresh Thai basil, finely chopped (optional)

a pinch of salt

2 bananas, cut in half lengthways

½ pineapple, cut into slices

**To serve**

4 spring onions (scallions), thinly sliced

2 tomatoes, cut into wedges

½ cucumber, cut into batons

a handful of fresh coriander (cilantro) leaves

a handful of Crispy Fried Shallots (green onions) (p.48) or crispy fried Thai shallots (p.74)

**1** Place a wok over medium heat and warm 2 tbsp of the coconut oil, then stir in the curry paste and fry until aromatic.

**2** Add the green beans and carrot and sauté for a couple of minutes, then add the rice and cook for another couple of minutes, stirring constantly. Once the rice starts to heat up, add the shallots then the kecap manis, tamari, red chillies, Thai basil, if using, and salt and continue to cook until the rice is hot through.

**3** Meanwhile, put a frying pan over a medium heat and warm the remaining coconut oil. Add the bananas and pineapple and sauté on both sides until they've taken on a bit of colour. Set aside.

**4** Transfer the fried rice to bowls and top each one with a slice of the sautéed banana and a couple of sautéed pineapple slices. Garnish with a choice of the spring onions, tomato, cucumber, coriander and Crispy Fried Shallots and serve.

# Raw futomaki

SERVES 4
WF | GF | RAW

Futomaki are long, thick rolls of sushi cased in a thin sheet of nori. The rolls often contain no fish and are instead filled with different-coloured vegetables, so they're ideal for vegans. Ensuring the ingredients don't just taste great but complement each other in the looks department is essential to the art of sushi making. Sushi chefs in Japan train for countless years, often spending over a year just on the rice – they'd probably never forgive this raw version where sushi rice is substituted with parsnips! We think the raw rolls look and taste great, plus they're packed with nutrition. If you're not sure how to roll sushi, have a look online – you'll find lots of helpful clips and tips. Umeboshi are small fermented Japanese plums that have been found to contain a lot of probiotics. They are available in a paste form in many health-food stores, but it's not a problem to omit them if they prove too hard to track down.

4 parsnips, peeled and cut into rough chunks

a handful of pine nuts

a pinch of salt

a dash of apple cider vinegar

1 bunch of fresh chives, finely cut

a dash of toasted sesame oil

4 sheets nori

½ tsp umeboshi paste (optional)

1 avocado, peeled, stoned and sliced

½ cucumber, sliced

50g/1¾oz rocket

1 red (bell) pepper, deseeded and thinly sliced

4 tbsp shoyu (make sure it's gluten free)

4 tbsp mirin

wasabi to serve

pickled ginger to serve

**1** Roughly process the parsnips in a food processor until they begin to resemble rice grains. Add the pine nuts at the last minute and pulse once or twice more. Put the mix in a bowl and season with the salt, cider vinegar, chives and sesame oil.

**2** On a sushi mat, place a sheet of nori, shiny side down, and pat down the parsnip rice to cover the bottom half of the sheet horizontally, about 0.5cm/¼in high. With your finger, very gently spread a thin layer of the umeboshi paste, if using, over the rice. Lay one-quarter of the avocado, cucumber, rocket and red pepper in the middle of the rice and begin to roll the sushi away from you. Just before you complete the roll, dampen the exposed nori slightly using your fingers, then complete the roll. Have a quick look online if you're not sure about how to do the rolling process. Repeat for the other three sheets.

**3** Once you have your rolls, use a sharp knife to cut them into round, even, bite-sized pieces.

**4** Mix the shoyu and mirin to form a dipping sauce and serve the futomaki with wasabi and pickled ginger.

# Tempeh and broccoli stir-fry

SERVES 4
WF | GF

This is a quick and easy but very nutritious everyday meal. Tempeh is a traditional soy product, originally from Indonesia, that is made using a fermentation process that binds the soya beans into a patty form. Alongside all the digestive benefits created by the fermentation process, tempeh is also a fantastic source of protein, fibre and many other vitamins. You should be able to find it in most good health-food stores.

1 butternut squash, peeled and cut into 1cm (½in) cubes

2 tbsp coconut oil (or cooking oil of your choice)

3 tbsp brown sugar

1 tsp ground cinnamon

about 225g/8oz/⅔ block tempeh, crumbled

1 leek, thinly sliced

1 head of broccoli, cut into small florets

1 red chilli, deseeded and sliced

60ml/2fl oz/¼ cup water

3 tbsp tamari (make sure it's gluten free)

3 tbsp pumpkin seeds

1 tbsp pumpkin seed oil

salt and pepper

cooked brown rice to serve

**1** Preheat the oven to 200°C/400°F/gas mark 6. In a bowl, mix the squash cubes with 1 tbsp of the coconut oil, 2 tbsp of the brown sugar, the cinnamon and a little salt and pepper. Place on a baking sheet and roast for 25–30 minutes, giving it a gentle stir every 10 minutes or so.

**2** When the squash is nearly ready, heat a wok, then add the remaining coconut oil and the tempeh. Cook on a high heat until the tempeh begins to turn golden, adding a splash of water if the wok is getting too dry. Add the leek and continue to cook for 2 minutes before adding the broccoli and chilli. Make sure you keep moving the wok to mix everything in.

**3** Add the water, the remaining sugar, the tamari and pumpkin seeds and fry for a further 3–5 minutes until the broccoli is nice and tender. Finish by stirring in the roasted butternut squash and the pumpkin seed oil and serve with brown rice.

# Raw phad thai

SERVES 4
WF | GF | RAW

This has got to be one of the most popular Thai dishes and it's easy to see why. It's a riot of colours and flavours, and no visit to Thailand would be complete without a visit to one of the many markets to sample this street-food staple. Just beware if you're veggie or vegan, though, as fish sauce is normally involved unless you very specifically ask for it not to be. In adapting this dish for a raw-food diet, courgettes replace the rice noodles (so it's also wheat- and gluten-free), but you could also use young coconut if you're able to get hold of it. If possible, a mandolin slicer for these vegetables is readily available and really works well to save time and create a better noodle effect, but be careful with it and use the safety guard!

**1** Put all the sauce ingredients in a blender and blend on high speed until smooth. Set aside.

**2** Put all the vegetable ribbons in a large bowl and mix through the sauce. Pile as high as you can on a large plate or bowl, and top with bean sprouts and coriander. Add all the other garnishes around the side of the plate, if you like, and serve.

### For the sauce
1 medjool date, pitted
1 heaped tbsp raw almond butter
2 sun-dried tomatoes
50ml/2fl oz/½ cup olive oil
2 tbsp tamari (make sure it's gluten free)
½ garlic clove
1cm/½in fresh root ginger, peeled
1 tbsp + 2 tsp agave syrup (or raw sweetener)
a pinch of sea salt
1 long red chilli, deseeded
juice of ½ lemon
1 tbsp + 1 tsp tamarind paste or juice

### For the vegetables
1 courgette (zucchini), finely sliced into ribbons
2 carrots, finely sliced
½ red onion, finely sliced
1 green dessert apple, cored and finely sliced
1 mango, peeled, stoned and finely sliced
a handful of bean sprouts
1 red (bell) pepper, deseeded and finely sliced
250g/9oz/2 cups mangetout (snow peas), sliced
250g/9oz/1 cup baby corn, finely sliced

### To garnish
bean sprouts
fresh coriander (cilantro)
lime wedges
chopped red chillies, sprouted mung beans, crushed raw almonds, trimmed spring onions (scallions) (optional)

# Smoky Mexican cowboy beans

SERVES 4
WF | GF

Otherwise known as frijoles charros, this is a classic way of serving beans in Mexico, and it makes a great alternative to refried beans. The smokiness usually comes from bacon, but we've recreated it using a combination of chipotle chilli, smoked paprika and wood-smoked onion. We love these beans served with a side of Guacamole (p.120) and some brown rice or quinoa.

115g/4oz/1 cup hickory, oak or mesquite woodchips (readily available online or in most cookery stores)

1 large white onion, chopped

1 red (bell) pepper

2 tbsp coconut oil (or cooking oil of your choice)

2 dried chipotle, soaked and chopped

2 garlic cloves, thinly sliced

½ tsp ground cumin

a pinch of salt

½ tsp smoked paprika

2 tbsp tomato purée

400g/14oz tinned chopped tomatoes

2 x 400g/14oz tins pinto beans, drained and rinsed

a handful of fresh coriander (cilantro), chopped to serve

2 limes, halved to serve

**1** Put the woodchips in a medium-sized saucepan. (Don't use your best one, as there may be some discoloration from this process.) Put a round piece of foil, with a few skewer holes in it, on top of the woodchips (make sure it reaches the sides of the pan so that the onion doesn't fall in), then put the onion on top of the foil and cover with a lid. Place on a high heat and smoke for 5–7 minutes. Remove one piece of onion to check that it's fully smoked (you can tell by the smell). If not, place back on the heat for another couple of minutes.

**2** Poke a few holes in the red pepper, then put it directly on an open gas flame until completely blackened, turning every minute or so. Put the blackened pepper in a container with a tight lid and leave to sweat for 10 minutes. Alternatively, preheat the grill (broiler) to 200°C/400°F before putting the stabbed pepper on a baking tray and placing it under the grill, moving it around occasionally, until it's evenly burnt all over. This should take about 10 minutes. By this time you should be able to remove the black skin easily. Cut the skinned pepper in half, remove the seeds, then slice the flesh.

**3** Heat the coconut oil in a saucepan and when hot, add the smoked onion and cook until translucent before adding the chipotle chillies, garlic, cumin, salt and smoked paprika. Continue to cook for a couple of minutes, stirring continuously, before adding the tomato purée. Cook again for a couple of minutes, then add the chopped tomatoes, sliced red pepper and pinto beans. Bring this to the boil and simmer for about 30 minutes.

**4** Garnish with chopped coriander and and serve with lime wedges.

# Seitan market plate

SERVES 2

This recipe showcases seitan in all its glory and is a favourite of ours for Sunday lunch, with its lovely chewy texture.

1 batch Seitan (p.172)
2 litres/68fl oz/2 quarts Vegetable Stock, homemade (p.170) or store-bought
1 tbsp tamari or soy sauce
1 tbsp Dijon mustard
1 tsp finely chopped fresh thyme leaves

**For the sweet potato mash**
6 sweet potatoes
1 knob vegan margarine or spread
salt and pepper

**For the roasted vegetables**
4 garlic cloves, unpeeled
4 parsnips, cut into wedges
3 carrots, cut into batons
2 tbsp olive oil
2 tsp chopped fresh rosemary leaves
10 cherry tomatoes, on the vine

**For the mushroom gravy**
1 tbsp vegetable oil
1 onion, chopped
1 garlic clove, chopped
1 glass red wine
125g/4½oz/2 cups button mushrooms, sliced
vegetable stock reserved from the Seitan
1 tbsp cornflour (cornstarch)

**To serve**
1 batch Flash-steamed Greens (p.116) or steamed purple-sprouting broccoli

1 Put the dough, stock and tamari in a large pan and bring to the boil. Reduce the heat and simmer, covered, for about 35–40 minutes until the dough has a soft, aerated texture, stirring every 10 minutes or so to keep it submerged. Drain the dough in a colander set over a bowl, reserving the stock for the mushroom gravy.

2 To make the mash, preheat the oven to 200°C/400°F/gas mark 6. Prick the sweet potatoes with a fork, then place on a baking tray and bake for around 45 minutes. For the roasted veggies, spread the garlic, parsnips and carrots in a roasting tin, drizzle with the oil and sprinkle with the rosemary. Season with salt and pepper and bake in the oven for the final 25 minutes of the sweet potato cooking time.

3 When the potatoes are ready, leave to cool slightly, then cut them in half and scoop the flesh into a pan. Put the pan over a medium heat, add the vegan margarine, season with salt and pepper and mash until smooth. Keep warm.

4 Next, put the dough in a roasting tin lined with greaseproof (waxed) paper. Coat the dough with the mustard, using a pastry brush, then sprinkle the thyme over the top. Place in the oven with the vegetables and roast both for a further 15–20 minutes until the mustard has formed a slight crust. Add the cherry tomatoes to the roasting vegetables for the final 10 minutes of the cooking time.

5 Meanwhile, make the gravy. Heat the oil in a pan over a medium heat and cook the onion and garlic until they start to turn golden. Add the red wine, and continue to cook until it has almost evaporated, then add the mushrooms and sauté until soft. Pour in the stock and simmer for another 15 minutes. Add the cornflour and cook for another minute or so until thickened.

6 Cut the seitan into slices and serve on a bed of sweet potato mash with the roasted vegetables, Flash-steamed Greens and a drizzle of mushroom gravy.

SERVES 4
WF | GF
OPTION

4 large wheat flour tortillas (omit
for wheat- and gluten-free)

1 batch each Tomato Salsa
and Guacamole (p.120)

1 batch sour Raw Cashew Cream (p.141)

300g/10½oz/1½ cups short-grained brown
rice, cooked (this is great for leftovers)

½ bunch of fresh coriander (cilantro)

2 limes, halved

**For the chipotle sauce**

4 dried chipotle chillies

2 dried red chillies

4 garlic cloves

250ml/9fl oz/1 cup + 2 tbsp water

225ml/8fl oz/1 cup orange juice

3 tbsp apple cider vinegar

2 tbsp brown sugar

1 tsp cacao powder or cocoa

½ tsp salt

½ tsp cayenne pepper

½ tsp ground cumin

¼ tsp ground cloves

**For the refried black beans**

1 onion, finely chopped

olive oil, for sautéing

1 garlic clove, chopped

½ chipotle chilli, soaked and chopped

½ tsp ground cumin

a pinch of ground cinnamon

400g/14oz/2 cups black beans,
drained and rinsed

# Burrito

An ingenious Mexican-American dish, the much-loved burrito is an easy-to-make, easy-to-eat dish. Distinguished from a taco by its size and by the fact that it's wrapped to enclose the filling, you can't beat it for a hearty lunch. Our Whitecross Street neighbour, Luardos, does a mean veggie one from its van. The popular burrito bowl is an ideal way to enjoy this dish for those avoiding wheat and gluten. Simply serve all the components in a large bowl instead of a wrap; we love to add some corn chips on the side.

**1** To make the sauce, preheat the oven to 200°C/400°F/gas mark 6. Put the chillies and garlic on a baking sheet. Roast the chillies for 1–2 minutes, taking care that they don't burn. Remove the chillies from the oven and place in a bowl of water to soften. Roast the garlic for 15–20 minutes. When the garlic is ready, remove it from the oven and remove the skins.

**2** Put all the sauce ingredients in a blender and combine until they're puréed. Put the purée in a pan, bring to the boil and simmer for 20 minutes until the mixture has reduced to a relatively thick sauce.

**3** To make the refried beans, sauté the onion in a little oil for a couple of minutes until translucent. Add the garlic, chipotle, cumin and cinnamon and sauté for a further couple of minutes, then add the black beans. Continue to cook for about 10 minutes, crushing them as they cook with a potato masher.

**4** To assemble the finished burritos, place the tortillas flat on a board. Off-centre, layer the rice, refried beans, Tomato Salsa, Guacamole, sour Raw Cashew Cream and chipotle sauce. Top with some coriander and a generous squeeze of lime juice and you're ready to roll!

**5** There are many techniques for rolling a burrito, but we normally just bring the bottom over, then tuck the sides in and finish the roll. We sometimes use a little water to help it stick together.

**6** Finally, heat a dry pan and lightly toast each burrito for about a minute on each side, then serve with lime wedges for squeezing over.

# Black bean tofu

David's very proud of his black bean sauce and it's been finely honed over many years. Widely used throughout China, it is known as douchi and doesn't actually use black beans at all. Instead, it's a cooking sauce made from fermented soya beans, which become black as a result of the enzymes released during the fermentation process. You'll find them in any Chinese grocery store and they're super-easy to work with. Here we're using the sauce with tofu, but it's extremely versatile and is great with any stir-fried or steamed dish.

### For the sauce

2 tbsp vegetable oil

1 white onion, roughly chopped

3 garlic cloves, finely chopped

1 long red chilli, deseeded and finely chopped

1 tbsp brown sugar

15g/½oz fresh root ginger, peeled and finely chopped

2 tbsp Shaoxing wine

3 tbsp tamari (make sure it's gluten free)

4 tbsp fermented black beans, rinsed and mashed

350ml/12fl oz/1½ cups Vegetable Stock (p.170) or ready-made vegetable stock

1 tbsp cornflour (cornstarch), mixed with 2 tbsp water to make a paste

### For the rest

1 green (bell) pepper, deseeded and diced

1 red (bell) pepper, deseeded and diced

2 tbsp vegetable oil

1 bunch of asparagus, cut into 2cm/¾in batons

½ bunch of spring onions (scallions), finely chopped

2 handfuls of bean sprouts

350g/12oz/1 block fresh firm tofu, cut into 2cm/¾in cubes

2 heads pak choy, cut in half

350g/12oz/2⅓ cups short-grain brown rice

8 sprigs fresh coriander (cilantro) to garnish

**1** To make the sauce, heat the vegetable oil in a pan, add the onion and sauté for about 3 minutes until it starts to turn golden. Add the garlic, chilli, sugar, ginger, Shaoxing wine, tamari and black beans and continue to sauté for a further 4–5 minutes before adding the vegetable stock. Bring to the boil and cook on a high heat for about 2 minutes. Add the cornflour paste and stir for a couple of minutes until the sauce has thickened. Remove from the heat and set aside.

**2** Place a wok over the highest heat until it's extremely hot. Add the peppers, then the vegetable oil and cook until they start to take on a little colour. Add all the other vegetables, except the pak choy. Add the tofu and continue to cook on a high heat for a further 3-4 minutes to get a bit of colour on everything. Turn down the heat before adding the black bean sauce so that it coats all the vegetables.

**3** Meanwhile, steam the rice for about 10 minutes until just tender, and the pak choy for about 7 minutes until wilted.

**4** Lay half a pak choy head on each plate and top with the black bean and tofu mixture. Garnish with coriander and serve with the steamed brown rice.

# 'Pulled' jackfruit sliders

Jackfruit is a strange-looking Asian fruit, and is not to be confused with its lookalike durian. It's easiest to deal with in canned form – just make sure it's canned in water not syrup! We couldn't believe how closely it resembles pulled meat when we first experimented with it; even the chap who sells pulled pork wraps next to us at the market was pretty keen on it!

**For the pulled jackfruit**

4 tbsp olive oil

2 small onions, chopped

4 garlic cloves, crushed

2 cans jackfruit, in water, drained and cut into quarters

800ml/28fl oz/3½ cups Vegetable Stock, homemade (p.170) or store-bought

2 tsp chopped fresh thyme leaves

1 chipotle chilli, soaked and chopped

2 tbsp apple cider vinegar

2 tsp tamari

2 tbsp molasses

½ tsp mustard powder

salt and pepper

**For the barbecue sauce**

1 tbsp olive oil

3 garlic cloves, crushed

1 small onion, chopped

2 tbsp chopped fresh thyme leaves

1 tbsp molasses

1 chipotle chilli, soaked and chopped

2 tbsp rum

2 tsp red wine vinegar

2 tbsp tamari (make sure it's gluten free)

300ml/10fl oz/1¼ cups tomato ketchup

**To serve**

1 batch Asian Slaw (p.79)

4 buns, halved

**1** For the pulled jackfruit, gently heat the olive oil in a pan. Sauté the onions for 2 minutes, then add the garlic and jackfruit and sauté for a further 10 minutes. Add all of the remaining ingredients, season and stir well. Bring to the boil, then simmer, covered, for 35–40 minutes. Check on the mixture every 10 minutes or so to make sure it isn't sticking to the bottom of the pan.

**2** If there is any liquid left after 40 minutes, remove the lid and cook until it evaporates. With a potato masher, lightly mash the jackfruit until it starts to break apart and resemble pulled meat. Remove from the heat and leave to one side.

**3** Meanwhile, make the barbecue sauce. Heat the oil in a pan over a medium heat. Add the garlic, onion and thyme and sauté for 2 minutes, then add the molasses and chipotle and leave to caramelize for 1–2 minutes. Add the rum, red wine vinegar and tamari and cook for a further 2 minutes. Pour in the ketchup, mix well and bring to the boil. Reduce the heat and simmer for 10–15 minutes until thick.

**4** Return the jackfruit pan to a gently heat. When it starts to gain some colour, spoon over 4–5 tbsp of the sauce. Mix well and cook until hot through.

**5** Load the buns with plenty of jackfruit, an extra dollop of sauce and a spoonful of Asian Slaw and serve.

# Farinata

Made with chickpea flour and olive oil, these traditional Italian pancakes are a wonderful option for vegans and those following a wheat- and gluten-free diet. They're also common in the south of France, where they're known as socca and eaten as street food, cooked on huge tin-plated copper skillets and seasoned with just a little salt and pepper. We've made this into a main meal by adding a delicious wild mushroom filling and a few other bits and pieces, but the crêpes are also delicious as a snack on their own.

**For the farinata batter**

375ml/13fl oz/1⅓ cups water

175ml/6fl oz/¾ cup extra-virgin olive oil, plus a little extra for cooking

200g/7oz/1½ cups chickpea flour (gram flour)

1 tbsp chopped fresh rosemary leaves

salt and pepper

**For the filling**

2 tbsp olive oil, plus a little extra for the tomatoes

½ onion, finely chopped

2 garlic cloves, finely chopped

150g/5½oz/2 cups wild mushrooms (we love porcini), sliced

150g/5½oz/2 cups button mushrooms, sliced

salt and pepper

½ bunch of fresh flat-leaf parsley, chopped, plus extra to garnish

**For the rest**

250g/9oz/1⅔ cups cherry tomatoes on the vine

olive oil

4 handfuls of rocket

1 tsp smoked paprika

1 batch Aioli (p.168)

**1** Put all the batter ingredients in a blender and combine for about 30 seconds on fast until smooth – don't worry if there are a few bubbles. Set aside to rest for about 30 minutes.

**2** To make the filling, heat the olive oil in a pan, then add the onion and garlic and sauté for a couple of minutes on a high heat. Add the mushrooms and seasoning and continue to sauté for a further 4–5 minutes. Finish off with the chopped parsley and set aside.

**3** Meanwhile, preheat the oven to 200°C/400°F/gas mark 6. Put the cherry tomatoes on a baking sheet with a drizzle of olive oil and some salt and pepper and roast for about 10 minutes until nicely coloured.

**4** Heat a little olive oil in a non-stick frying pan over a medium heat. Pour one-quarter of the batter into the pan and swirl round to cover the base. Fry for a few minutes until golden, then flip over and fry the other side. Remove from the pan and keep warm while you repeat with the remaining batter.

**5** Place the farinata on individual plates, spoon the mushroom filling on top, then fold over to cover. Sprinkle with a little paprika. Serve with the roasted tomatoes, some rocket and a spoonful of Aioli.

SERVES 4
WF

# Pearl barley risotto
## with pumpkin and sage

Is there anything more comforting than risotto? Our version uses pearl barley rather than arborio rice for a new take on this classic, but the soaked cashews and nutritional yeast still provide the essential cheesy creaminess. Pearl barley has a delicious slightly nutty taste and is a wonderfully healthy wholegrain, high in both fibre and protein. This dish is fantastic served with our Flash-steamed Greens (p.116) or a light green salad.

300g/10½oz/scant 1¼ cups pumpkin, cubed

75ml/2½fl oz/generous ¼ cup olive oil

1 large onion, finely chopped

2 garlic cloves, finely chopped

100g/3½oz/¾ cup cashews, soaked for at least 2 hours

125ml/4fl oz/½ cup Soya Milk, homemade (p.157) or store-bought

3 tbsp nutritional yeast

2 litres/3½ pints/2 quarts Vegetable Stock, homemade (p.170) or store-bought

300g/10½oz/1½ cups pearl barley, rinsed

125ml/4fl oz/½ cup white wine

4 fresh sage leaves, roughly chopped, plus 4 leaves for garnish

a pinch of freshly grated nutmeg

salt and pepper

½ bunch of fresh chives, chopped, to garnish

**1** Preheat the oven to 200°C/400°F/gas mark 6. Put the pumpkin cubes on a baking sheet, drizzle with 2 tbsp of the olive oil and add a little salt and pepper. Roast in the oven for about 30 minutes, or until golden. Remove and leave to cool.

**2** Meanwhile, heat 2 tbsp of the olive oil in a pan and sauté half the onion for a couple of minutes until translucent. Add 1 clove of garlic and continue to sauté for a further 2 minutes before adding the wine, cashews, milk, nutritional yeast, a pinch of salt and pepper and 200ml/7fl oz/scant 1 cup of the vegetable stock. Bring to the boil, reduce the heat and simmer for about 10 minutes.

**3** Leave to cool for 15 minutes, then transfer to a blender along with half of the roasted pumpkin. (Be careful as the mixture might still be hot. Using the pulse function is a good way to keep control, lifting the lid occasionally to release any steam build-up). Pulse until the mixture is very smooth.

**4** Put the barley and the rest of the vegetable stock in a pan and bring to the boil. Reduce the heat and simmer for about 30 minutes, or until most of the stock has been absorbed and the barley is soft. Strain and leave to cool.

**5** Heat 1 tbsp of the oil in a pan and sauté the remaining onion and garlic until translucent. Add the cashew mix and carefully bring to the boil, stirring continuously. If you find it's a bit too thick, just add a little water. Add the barley and the other half of the roasted pumpkin and continue to cook, stirring often. Add the sage and nutmeg and continue to cook for a further 5 minutes before checking the seasoning and adding a little more salt and pepper if needed. Serve in large bowls, garnished with chopped chives and a leaf of sage.

# Raw 'lasagne'

The layers of this lasagne look so colourful and fresh and it's absolutely packed with vitamins and nutrients. The dish is at its best when the vegetables are sliced into paper-thin strips with a mandolin – you can make do without one, but they're an inexpensive and very worthwhile investment for raw food fans. The walnut pâté is a great recipe on its own, too, as a raw pâté or spread.

2 plum tomatoes, sliced

1 batch Walnut Pâté (p.143)

1 batch Green Pesto (p.167)

1 batch Marinara Sauce (p.169)

3 courgettes (zucchini), very thinly sliced to resemble lasagne sheets

2 handfuls pea shoots or micro-herbs to garnish

**For the sweetcorn (corn) sauce**

1 sweetcorn (corn) cob, kernels removed

4 tbsp olive oil

4 tbsp water

½ tsp cayenne pepper

salt and pepper

**1** In a blender, combine all the sauce ingredients until smooth. Pass through a fine sieve and adjust the seasoning to taste.

**2** To put the dish together, put a 10cm/4in catering ring on a flat plate or board. Layer one quarter of the components, starting with 3 slices of tomato, then the Walnut Pâté, Green Pesto, Marinara Sauce and courgettes. Repeat the layering until the ring is full, making sure courgette is your final layer.

**3** Remove the ring and repeat to make the other three lasagnes. Put a little of the sweetcorn sauce on the side of each plate, top the lasagnes with pea shoots or micro-herbs and serve.

# Chocolate chilli mole
## with black beans

We absolutely love using sweet ingredients in savoury dishes, and the dark chocolate used in this classic Mexican dish counterbalances the intensity of the chilli brilliantly. It also lends the sauce its dark colour and intense richness. This is traditionally served over meat, but we've opted for vegetables and black beans to create a hearty vegan meal. Serve with brown rice or quinoa, some steamed greens and our Tomato Salsa (p.120).

**For the spice mix**

2 tbsp sesame seeds

1 chipotle chilli, soaked and roughly chopped

45g/1½oz/⅓ cup almonds, roughly chopped

6 tortilla chips, crumbled

1 tsp ground cinnamon

½ tsp ground cumin

**For the sauce**

2 sweet potatoes, diced

1 tbsp olive oil

2 sweetcorn (corn) cobs

1 onion, chopped

1 tbsp vegetable oil (or cooking oil of your choice)

4 garlic cloves, chopped

500ml/17fl oz/generous 2 cups Vegetable Stock, homemade (p.170) or store-bought

2 tbsp peanut butter

400g/14oz tinned chopped tomatoes

70g/2½oz dark chocolate (make sure it's vegan and has a high cacao content)

400g/14oz/2 cups black beans, drained and rinsed

1 courgette (zucchini), cubed

cooked brown rice or quinoa to serve

salt

**1** Preheat the oven to 200°C/400°F/gas mark 6. Place the diced sweet potatoes on a baking sheet, drizzle with the olive oil and roast for about 20 minutes.

**2** Meanwhile, make the spice mix. In a dry pan, lightly toast the sesame seeds, chilli, almonds and tortilla chips. Transfer to a blender (or use a traditional pestle and mortar), adding the spices and blending until it's as smooth as possible.

**3** Put the sweetcorn on the open flame of a gas hob, turning occasionally, until they're a bit blackened all the way around. Alternatively, preheat a grill (broiler) to 200°C/400°F before putting the corn on a baking tray and placing it under the grill, moving the ears around occasionally until they're lightly browned all over. This should take about 10 minutes. Remove from the heat and set aside to cool before removing the kernels.

**4** Sauté the onion with the vegetable oil until translucent, then add the garlic and continue to sauté for a further 2–3 minutes. Add the vegetable stock, peanut butter, spice mix and tinned tomatoes and bring to the boil. Remove from the heat and allow to cool a little, then transfer to the blender and pulse until smooth.

**5** Return the mixture to the pan and return to the heat, adding the dark chocolate and the black beans. Heat for a couple of minutes, then add the corn kernels, courgette and roasted sweet potato. Bring to the boil while continuously stirring, then simmer for a further 15 minutes or so while you cook some rice or quinoa. Season to taste and serve.

SIDES
& DIPS

# Asian greens with vegan 'oyster' sauce

We love to add a whack of greens to pretty much every meal we eat, and this is a great way to do it. Buy whatever's available – pak choy is increasingly easy to get hold of and available in most supermarkets, but gai lan is a big favourite of ours if you're able to get to an oriental grocery. Vegan 'oyster' sauce is just as tasty with local greens like chard, kale or cabbage and is also lovely with stir-fries like our Tempeh and Broccoli Stir-fry (p.97).

your choice of greens – pak choy, gai lan or morning glory are all good

**For the oyster sauce**

1 tbsp coconut oil (or cooking oil of your choice)

½ onion, finely chopped

4 cloves garlic, finely chopped

1 tbsp sugar

4 tbsp Shaoxing wine

1–2 tbsp tamari, to taste (make sure it's gluten free)

a dash of toasted sesame oil

**1** Heat the coconut oil in a pan and sauté the onion and garlic over a medium heat for a few minutes until they become translucent. Add the sugar and continue to heat until it begins to caramelize, about 4 minutes, then add the wine and flambé (if you can and want to show off a bit – otherwise not the end of the world to just cook it). Taste and add the tamari and a dash of sesame oil to season.

**2** Steam the greens. How long will depend on which greens you're using, but it normally takes about 5 minutes.

**3** Drain, transfer to a bowl or plate, pour the sauce over the top and serve.

SERVES 4
WF | GF

# Flash-steamed greens

We use this technique for cooking the greens in our Buddha Bowls – our British Street Food Award-winning signature dish! They are nutritionally well-rounded meals made up of all our favourite things – Massaman curry (p.84), Carrot and Kimchi Pickle (p.145), flash steamed kale or other greens, shortgrain brown rice and some omega seed sprinkle. They're always a hit at events and the fact that we still enjoy them despite having them at least weekly for the last 5 years makes us think we're onto a good thing! This recipe is very simple and very fast, and people love watching their food being steamed in front of them. It's also a great way of avoiding soggy greens!

200g/7oz/4 cups kale, spring greens or savoy cabbage • sea salt and cracked black pepper

**1** Heat a dry wok or frying pan until very hot, then add the greens and a ladle of hot water, which will instantly steam them.

**2** After about 10 seconds, they will be ready to serve with a little salt and cracked black pepper.

# Sunomono

Sunomono is a cool, crisp Japanese cucumber salad. It's tangy, sweet, healthy and incredibly easy to make. Often served as an accompaniment to sushi, it's ideal as a side dish, although it can also be served on its own as a light starter.

1 cucumber • ¼ tsp sea salt • 4 tbsp rice wine vinegar (brown if possible) • 1 tbsp brown sugar • ½ tsp tamari (make sure it's gluten free) • 2 tbsp sesame seeds • 3g wakame, soaked if dried

Slice the cucumber as thinly as possible. Place the slices in a bowl and mix in the salt, leaving it to sit for about 5 minutes. Meanwhile, mix the vinegar, sugar and tamari together until the sugar dissolves. Squeeze out any excess water from the cucumber, then add the vinegar mixture, seeds, and wakame. Mix well and serve.

MAKES
8–10 SLICES
WF | GF

# Maple-glazed tofu

Easy to make and unbelievably yummy, these tofu slices can be added to a variety of dishes to add a protein element. We love serving them with some brown rice, steamed broccoli and a side of Miso Soup (p.33), but they're also great on top of curries, in salads or even on their own as a snack.

2 tbsp maple syrup • 30g/1oz fresh root ginger, peeled and finely chopped • 2½ tbsp tamari (make sure it's gluten free) • 350g/12oz/1 block firm tofu, cut into 8–10 slices

Preheat the oven to 180°C/350°F/gas mark 4. Mix the maple syrup, ginger and tamari in a bowl. Line a baking sheet with greaseproof (waxed) paper and put the tofu slices on it. Pour the maple glaze over the slices and place the sheet in the oven for 15 minutes. Flip the tofu slices over, bake for a further 10 minutes until golden brown and serve.

# Baba ganoush

SERVES 4
WF | GF

This wonderfully smoky charred aubergine dip is popular throughout the Middle East. The sweetness of the pomegranate seeds works brilliantly, and they look so beautiful as a garnish, sparkling like rubies. A good tip for removing the pomegranate seeds is to cut the pomegranate in half horizontally, then, taking one half at a time, hold it firmly over a bowl and bash the back with a wooden spoon to dislodge the seeds. We love to serve it with flatbreads and vegetable crudités alongside hummus, pickles, olives and other Middle Eastern favourites.

2 aubergines (eggplant)

3 tbsp tahini

juice of ½ lemon

½ garlic clove, finely chopped

2 tbsp olive oil, plus extra to serve

1 cucumber, diced

a handful of chopped fresh parsley, plus extra to garnish

6 fresh mint leaves

1 pomegranate, deseeded

salt and pepper

**1** Carefully stab the aubergines with a small knife before placing them on the open flame of the hob for about 10 minutes to burn the skin all over. Turn them over occasionally so they are evenly burned. Alternatively, if using a grill (broiler), preheat it to 200°C/400°F before putting the stabbed aubergines on a baking tray and placing them under the grill, moving them around occasionally, until they're evenly burned all over. This should take about 10 minutes.

**2** When they're ready, put the aubergines into a metal container and wrap with clingfilm (plastic wrap) to make them sweat for about 30 minutes. At this point, open them up slightly and remove all the white flesh, avoiding the burned bits.

**3** Roughly chop the flesh, then mix well with the tahini, lemon juice, garlic, olive oil, diced cucumber, chopped parsley and mint until it resembles a dip.

**4** Adjust the seasoning to taste and garnish with pomegranate seeds, a little more parsley and a splash of olive oil.

# Guacamole

Flavourful yet simple and super-healthy, we have the Aztecs to thank for this fantastic classic dip. Guacamole is obviously delicious with tortilla chips or vegetable crudités, but we also put it in lots of our sandwiches and salads, and we serve it as a side with pretty much all of our Mexican dishes.

2 ripe avocados, peeled and stoned • ¼ red onion, chopped • ½ red chilli, deseeded and finely chopped • 10 sprigs fresh coriander (cilantro) • juice of ½ lime • salt and pepper

**1** Put everything in a food processor and blitz for about 10 seconds, making sure you keep some of the texture. If you feel like getting more hands on, do it the traditional way, using a pestle and mortar.

**2** Adjust the chilli, lime and salt and pepper to your taste.

# Tomato salsa

Proof that simple sometimes really is best, this tomato salsa (also known as pico de gallo) is practically a mandatory accompaniment to any Mexican dish. As with guacamole, we love it as a dip, but it also works brilliantly as a side dish – it's lime freshness enlivens all it accompanies!

½ red onion, chopped • 5 plum tomatoes, finely diced • ½ red chilli, deseeded and finely chopped, or more to taste • 10 sprigs fresh coriander (cilantro) • juice of ½ lime • a dash of olive oil • salt and pepper

Simply mix everything together thoroughly, and adjust the chilli, lime and salt and pepper to your taste.

DESSERTS

SERVES 2
WF | GF

# Poached pears

## with vanilla cashew cream

These spice-infused poached pears make a light yet intensely flavourful dessert. The recipe also works well with plums, figs, nectarines and cherries. If you want to make some up in advance, you can store the pears in the liquor in a sealed container in the fridge for a couple of days. This will really heighten the flavours, too, but it's not necessary if you want to enjoy them straight away.

750ml/26fl oz/3¼ cups water

80g/3oz/⅓ cup sugar

1 cinnamon stick

2 star anise

10–12 saffron strands

1 stick lemongrass, bruised a little to release the flavour

½ glass white wine (or red for a pink pear)

2 dessert pears, such as Conference pears, peeled

ground cinnamon to dust

1 batch sweet Raw Cashew Cream (p.141) to serve – try adding 1 pinch of saffron strands with the vanilla

**1** Put the water and sugar in a pan along with the cinnamon, star anise, saffron, lemongrass and white wine and bring to the boil, stirring occasionally to help dissolve the sugar.

**2** Meanwhile, peel the pears, then, using a knife or an apple corer, remove as much as you can of the core, keeping the pear intact and leaving its stalk untouched.

**3** Reduce the heat, add the pears, cover and simmer gently for 45 minutes. Turn off the heat, but leave the pears to sit in the poaching liquor for another 30–40 minutes to really take on the flavours.

**4** Carefully remove the pears from the poaching liquor. Set aside to cool, then transfer to the fridge. Keep some of the poaching liquor to serve.

**5** When they're nicely chilled, put each pear on a bed of Raw Cashew Cream. Lightly dust each one with cinnamon and serve with a little poaching liquor drizzled over the top.

MAKES 4
WF | GF

# Mango and blueberry chia seed pudding

Native to South America, chia seeds have been a vital part of Mayan and Aztec diets for centuries. Meaning 'strength' in Mayan, chia seeds were used as an energizing food and considered even more valuable than gold. Rich in omega-3, antioxidants, fibre and protein as well as countless other nutrients, it's easy to understand why. We use these seeds whenever we can: mixing them into drinks, sprinkling them over meals, using them as an egg replacer (they form a gel when mixed with water), or just making stand-alone chia dishes like this light, healthy dessert. It looks beautiful made in small clear jars.

250ml/9fl oz/generous 1 cup coconut milk

250ml/9fl oz/generous 1 cup Almond Milk, homemade (p.157) or store-bought

2 tbsp coconut palm nectar or agave syrup

7 tbsp chia seeds

1 large mango

250g/9oz/1⅔ cups blueberries

zest of 1 lime

**1** In a large bowl, mix together the two milks and the palm nectar. Add the chia seeds, mix well and leave for 10 minutes.

**2** Meanwhile, peel and remove the flesh from the mango. Dice half of the flesh and purée the rest. Mix the two and transfer one-quarter of the mixture to the bottom of each serving bowl or jar. Top with the chia mix and leave to set in the fridge – this should take about 1½–2 hours.

**3** When ready to serve, top with blueberries and lime zest and enjoy!

# Tropical fruit rice rollers
## with sweet coconut dipping sauce

A fun twist on the classic summer roll, this is a light, bright dessert that's a great alternative to a fruit salad. Use whatever tropical fruit you're able to find. Rice papers are increasingly easy to buy and a lot of supermarkets now stock them, but you'll definitely find them at Asian grocery stores.

8 round rice papers

a handful of fresh mint leaves, plus extra to garnish

1 mango, peeled, stoned and cut into equal-sized strips

1 firm papaya, cut into equal-sized strips

3 passion fruit, scooped out

1 pineapple, cut into equal-sized strips

¼ watermelon, cut into equal-sized strips

2 bananas, cut into equal-sized strips

**For the dipping sauce**

400ml/14fl oz/1¾ cups coconut milk

80g/3oz/⅓ cup palm sugar

1 tsp vanilla essence or seeds of ½ vanilla pod

**1** First make the dipping sauce by placing all the ingredients in a pan and bringing them to the boil. Reduce to a simmer and allow to reduce for about 5 minutes. Set aside to cool.

**2** Prepare to assemble the rollers by placing a slightly dampened tea towel on your kitchen table and also setting up a bowl of cold water large enough to hold a rice paper sheet. Make one at a time: first, submerge a rice paper sheet for about 10 seconds, then put it on the dampened tea towel and leave it for about 15 seconds before turning it over. Place a few mint leaves just off-centre (this will mean you're able to see them through the rolls, which looks rather pretty). Next, layer a little of each fruit, probably about 1 or 2 strips of each. (Make sure you're able to seal the rolls; you want them to be generously filled, but less is easier to roll and you do generally need less than you think in these matters. If you have any leftover fruit, you can always just pop it in the blender with some agave syrup and ice to whip up a quick smoothie!)

**3** Take the edge of the rice paper nearest to you and fold it over the fruit, tucking in the sides as you roll through. Once the roll is made, transfer it to a plate and cover with clingfilm (plastic wrap). Repeat. When the rolls are ready, put the plate in the fridge for a couple of hours or so.

**4** Serve with a ramekin of the dipping sauce and a little mint to garnish.

# Borage and blueberry snow cones

These are a novel take on a much-loved frozen dessert. We tend to enjoy these as a little afternoon treat on a hot day, but they're also great fun served as canapés or even as an amuse-bouche if you're getting fancy! Borage, or starflower as it's also known, has a light, cucumber-like taste that's hard to resist, but it's also packed with good nutrition, making it an all-round winner, especially when combined with antioxidant-rich blueberries. You'll be able to buy the borage online or from natural health-food stores, but you can also experiment making these with all kinds of different flavours, both sweet and savoury. We love to serve them in small metal tins, but you can also serve them in paper cones for more of a street-food vibe. The syrup will last for weeks in the fridge, making these easy to rustle up quickly when the sun pops out its head.

### For the syrup

200ml/7fl oz/scant 1 cup water

5 tbsp rice syrup

125g/4½oz/¾ cup fresh or frozen blueberries, save a few to garnish

50g/1¾oz borage, plus extra edible flowers to decorate

zest of 1 lemon

### For the snow

1–2 handfuls of ice per serving (if you can buy crushed ice, it will be easier on your blender)

**1** Put all the ingredients for the syrup in a pan and bring to the boil, stirring occasionally to prevent it from burning. Turn down to a medium heat and allow to reduce for about 15–20 minutes until the mixture has become slightly thick and syrupy.

**2** Transfer to a sealed jar in the fridge until you're ready to serve. (It's also a good idea to put your serving cups in the freezer as this point so they will hold the ice well when it's time to serve the snow cones.)

**3** Put the ice in a blender and blitz until nicely crushed. Quickly scoop the ice into your cups and spoon over a generous amount of the syrup. Garnish with a blueberry and extra edible flowers and serve.

SERVES 4
WF | GF

# Sago pudding

## with coconut milk, palm sugar and banana

This is a sweet pudding that can be eaten warm or cold. It is made by boiling sago with coconut milk and palm sugar. It always reminds us of being on holiday in Thailand, which is no bad thing! Sago itself is a starch derived from the centre of a palm stem and is a staple food for the tribes of New Guinea. We use pearl sago here, which is sago produced as small white, dry balls. It's vital to soak it before use for about two hours, during which time its soft, spongy nature will be revealed. It's not dissimilar to tapioca, but don't let crummy school dinners put you off trying it again.

1 litre/34fl oz/1 quart water

150g/5½oz pearl sago or tapioca, soaked and drained

a pinch of salt

70g/2½oz/¼ cup palm sugar

200ml/7fl oz/1 scant cup coconut milk

1 banana, sliced

sesame seeds, white or black, toasted, to garnish

1 Put the water in a pan along with the sago, salt and half the palm sugar and bring to the boil, stirring continuously. Simmer for about 20 minutes until the sago has gone transparent (don't worry if there are one or two white dots in the middle of the sago; it will still be cooked). Drain the water using a fine strainer and put the sago pearls to one side.

2 In a separate pan, bring the coconut milk and the remaining palm sugar to the boil, stirring so that the palm sugar dissolves. Add the banana and sago and simmer for a further 2–3 minutes. Spoon the pudding into bowls and sprinkle with sesame seeds. Enjoy immediately or allow to cool completely before chilling until ready to serve cold.

MAKES 20
WF | GF

# Peanut and black sesame sweet dumplings

Made with glutinous rice flour, these sweet dumplings have a wonderfully chewy texture, and their plain exterior belies a rich, nutty filling that oozes out as you bite in. Traditionally served at Chinese New Year, our preference is to have them on their own, rolled in ground peanuts, but for those with a sweet tooth, you can omit the extra peanuts and serve them in a sweet soup made from the liquid used to cook them in. (If you're doing the latter, try adding a bit more sugar, a star anise and some ginger to the cooking liquid, then cook to thicken.) You'll find glutinous rice flour in Asian grocers – surprisingly, it doesn't contain gluten!

### For the filling

30g/1¼oz black sesame seeds, toasted in a pan (be careful not to burn)

100g/3½oz/heaped ⅓ cup peanut butter

100g/3½oz/½ cup brown sugar, plus extra to taste

### For the dumplings

1 litre/34fl oz/1 quart water

250g/9oz/2 cups glutinous rice flour, plus extra to dust

80–100g/3–3½oz/½–scant 1 cup brown sugar

100g/3½oz/⅔ cup unsalted peanuts, roasted in the oven, then ground using a pestle and mortar

**1** First, make the filling. Grind the black sesame seeds using a pestle and mortar until powdered, then combine with the peanut butter and brown sugar in a bowl.

**2** Pour 200ml/7fl oz/scant 1 cup of the water over the rice flour and knead well until it forms a soft, sticky dough; if it's too wet, add more flour and if it's too dry, just add a little more water. Dust your hands and the table with some extra flour if it makes it easier to work with and roll the dough into a tube, about the width of a courgette (zucchini). Cut off approximately 1cm/½in pieces (each piece should weigh about 25g/1oz) and cover with a slightly dampened tea towel to prevent the dough from drying out. The dough must be used fresh.

**3** Flatten each piece so that it resembles a disc and gather this into a cup shape. Fill each with about ½ tsp of the filling and fold the top over, rolling between your hands so you get a smooth, round ball. Dust with a little more rice flour.

**4** Mix the remaining water with the sugar, stirring until the sugar has dissolved, then bring to the boil. Reduce the heat to a simmer and add the dumplings in batches – you should be able to do 5 or 6 at a time. Simmer for around 5 minutes, or until they rise to the surface. Don't overcook otherwise they will fall apart!

**5** Remove from the water using a slotted spoon, cool a little and roll in the ground peanuts. Serve immediately while warm.

SERVES 2–4

# Churros

## with dark chocolate dipping sauce

For when you need a treat, these long, piped Spanish-style doughnuts really fit the bill. Rolled in sugar and cinnamon and served with a dark chocolate sauce for dunking, this is the indulgent, delicious counterbalance to all the healthy stuff! In Spain they're even eaten for breakfast dipped in hot chocolate or coffee if you ever feel like an early morning sugar overload! A brilliant street-food staple, churros (especially from Churros Bros) are one of our favourite things to trade a Buddha Bowl (p.116) for when we're out at events! You'll need a piping bag for this one (ideally with a star nozzle).

**For the sugar dip**
75g/2½oz/⅔ cup brown sugar
a pinch of salt
½ heaped tbsp ground cinnamon

**For the churros**
250ml/9fl oz/1 cup + 2 tbsp water
a pinch of salt
2½ tbsp sugar
60ml/2fl oz/4 tbsp vegetable oil, plus an extra 500ml/17fl oz/2 cups for frying
1 tsp vanilla extract
110g/4oz/¾ cup plain (all-purpose) flour

**For the sauce**
100g/3½oz dark chocolate (make sure it's vegan and has a high cacao content)

**1** First, make the dip. Mix together the sugar, salt and cinnamon in a bowl. Set aside.

**2** Next, make the churros dough. In a pan, bring the water to the boil before adding the salt and sugar. Once they've dissolved, turn off the heat and add the oil and vanilla extract. Add the flour and mix thoroughly until all the ingredients are well combined. Transfer to a piping bag and set aside.

**3** To make the sauce. Use a bain marie (or put a glass bowl over a pot of simmering water). Add the chocolate and heat until melted.

**4** Heat the 400ml/14fl oz/1¾ cups oil in a pan until it reaches about 190°C/375°F, when a cube of bread browns in 60 seconds. Pipe in some long strands of the churros dough (you should be able to do about 4 at a time) and move them around so that they cook evenly. Remove when crispy and golden using a slotted spoon and roll in the sugar dip. Monitor the heat as you cook the remaining batches, keeping the cooked churros warm until you have used up all the dough.

**5** Serve the churros hot with the chocolate dipping sauce.

SERVES
6–8
WF | GF | RAW
OPTION

# Chocolate ganache

This has to be one of the most straightforward yet most rewarding raw desserts. It's smooth, rich, chocolatey and deeply satisfying. And it's healthy, as the raw cacao is a gold mine of antioxidants and other nutrients. It also contains chemicals such as serotonin and phenylethylamine, known to be mood-enhancers – so it won't just be the taste that makes you happy! The great thing about raw desserts is that you can generally just put them in the freezer for convenience. When you feel like a piece, simply remove the cake, leave it to thaw just enough to cut a slice, then pop it back in the freezer for future treats. The ganache filling also works well to make raw truffles. Simply roll it into balls and coat with your choice of desiccated coconut, raw cacao powder, cinnamon or anything that takes your fancy. To keep this completely raw, you do need a dehydrator for the crust, but if you don't have one, use an oven instead. Coconut oil melts at room temperature but you can speed up the process by placing it by a radiator or on top of your dehydrator.

### For the crust

150g/5½oz/1 cup pecans

150g/5½oz/1 cup almonds

80ml/2½fl oz/⅓ cup maple syrup, agave syrup or sweetener of your choice

100g/3½oz coconut oil (or cooking oil of your choice), melted

a pinch of salt

1 tsp ground cinnamon

a pinch of cayenne

### For the filling

170g/6oz raw tahini

100g/3½oz/⅔ cup medjool dates, deseeded

180ml/6fl oz/¾ cup agave syrup

100g/3½oz coconut oil, melted

a pinch of salt

½ tsp vanilla extract

200ml/7fl oz/1 scant cup water

200g/7oz/1¾ cups raw cacao powder

½ avocado, peeled and stoned

### To serve (optional)

250g/9oz/1⅔ cups mixed berries

**1** First, make the crust. Put the pecans and almonds in a bowl with the sweetener, then transfer them to a Teflex sheet, set your dehydrator to 45°C/113°F and dehydrate for about 12 hours, mixing the nuts around every few hours to make sure they're evenly dehydrated. If using an oven, preheat the oven to 160°C/325°F/ gas mark 3. Transfer the mix to a baking sheet and bake for 15–20 minutes, mixing every few minutes and being careful not to burn the nuts.

**2** When ready, transfer to a food processor, add the coconut oil, salt, cinnamon and cayenne and combine until the mixture resembles crunchy peanut butter. Line a 23cm/9in cake tin with greaseproof (waxed) paper. Press the mixture in to form a crust and chill.

**3** While the crust is chilling, make the filling by putting all the filling ingredients in a blender or food processor and blitzing until smooth. Adjust the sweetener to your preference. Pour the mixture into the cake tin and refrigerate until solid. Serve chilled with mixed berries, if you like.

# Raw chocolate brownies

MAKES 5–6
WF | GF | RAW

These raw brownies are super-moist and very moreish, but unlike normal brownies are also packed with nutrients as both raw cacao and lacuma (a Peruvian fruit, sold as powder that's a delicious, slightly vanilla like sweetener) are extremely rich in magnesium and antioxidants to name just a couple of their benefits. The palm nectar or agave is low-glycaemic, so you also won't get the usual sugar crash after having a couple of these! We find Tree Harvest a very good and reasonably priced supplier of many of our raw ingredients and they operate by mail order, but otherwise you should find everything we use in a good health-food store. You can make these yummy treats in just 5 minutes!

125g/2½oz/¾ cup medjool dates, pitted
100g/3½oz/⅔ cup pecans
4 tbsp unsweetened desiccated coconut
4 tbsp coconut palm or agave nectar
5 tbsp raw cacao powder, plus extra to dust
1 tsp lacuma powder (optional)
¼ tsp sea salt

**1** Put the dates in a food processor and grind just enough to form a paste. Add the pecans and continue to grind until they're all about the size of a rice grain.

**2** Add the coconut, palm nectar, cacao powder, lacuma, if using, and sea salt and mix thoroughly with a spoon. Shape into brownie-like squares and dust with cacao powder. They're ready to eat immediately if you can't resist, but they're also quite good chilled, so just put them in a sealed container in the fridge. They should keep for 4–5 days.

# Silken tofu chocolate mousse

## with raspberry coulis

Silken tofu is fantastic in vegan desserts. We use it a lot for cheesecakes as well as mousses, but make sure you do buy silken tofu and not one of the other varieties of tofu, as it will make a big difference. This really satisfies the craving for dessert but is much lower in fat and cholesterol than most regular puds, so it's an all-round winner!

110g/3½oz/¾ cup dark chocolate chips (make sure they are vegan and have a high cacao content)

300g/10½oz/scant 1 block firm silken tofu

75ml/2½fl oz/¼ cup + 1 tbsp maple syrup or agave nectar

1 tsp vanilla extract

250g/9oz/1⅔ cups raspberries

fresh mint leaves to garnish

**1** Melt the chocolate chips in a heatproof bowl set over a pan of gently simmering water.

**2** Pour into a blender, add the tofu, maple syrup or agave nectar and vanilla extract and blend until smooth. Pour into shot glasses, leaving a little room on the top for the coulis, and leave to chill and set in the fridge for about 2 hours.

**3** For the coulis, reserve a few whole raspberries for decoration, then push the remainder through a sieve into a bowl using a spoon.

**4** Top the shot glasses with some coulis and garnish with whole raspberries and mint. Serve chilled.

PICKLES,
SPREADS
& TREATS

MAKES
500G/1LB 2OZ
WF | GF
RAW

# Probiotic raw nut cheese

This is a delicious option if you're ever craving cheese, and it's wonderful served with grapes and crackers or as a spread. Experiment with the seasonings; we often add chopped herbs and shallots (green onions) to make a kind of herby cheese, or coat it with pink peppercorns. Here we've just used cashews, but you can experiment with other nuts, such as almonds or macadamias. Just buy any good-quality vegan probiotic powder from the nutritional supplement section of your health-food store; if you can't get powder, you can buy capsules and empty them. As with the nut milks (p.157) and cashew cream (opposite), you can make this in a normal blender but be careful not to burn it out – the longer the cashews have been soaked, the easier it will be. A high-speed blender such as a Vitamix would be the ideal tool for this process. This dish also has a range of digestive benefits and you can buy the nutritional yeast (the ingredient that really gives this its cheesy flavour) fortified with vitamin B12 – often lacking in a vegan diet.

500g/1lb 2oz/3⅔ cups raw cashews, soaked overnight or for a minimum of 8 hours

1 tsp probiotic powder

2 tbsp onion powder

1 tbsp garlic powder

4–5 tbsp nutritional yeast (make sure it's gluten free)

salt and pepper

**1** Drain the soaked cashews, then put them in a blender with the probiotic powder and blend until smooth.

**2** Transfer the mixture to a bowl and cover the top with clingfilm (plastic wrap), punching a few holes in the top so that the probiotics can breathe. Leave the bowl at room temperature for about 8–12 hours. You'll know the cheese is ready when it has grown in size and has taken on an aerated quality.

**3** Season to taste with the onion powder, garlic powder, nutritional yeast, salt and pepper. You can store the nut cheese in the fridge for up to 1 week.

MAKES
150G/5½OZ
WF | GF
RAW

# Raw cashew cream

## with sweet and sour variations

This cream has its origins in the raw-food movement but it is also a staple of a vegan diet because it is such an easy and delicious way to add that dairy feeling to a wide array of sweet and savoury dishes. You must use raw cashews in this recipe because in this natural state they have very little flavour of their own and simply lend creaminess while taking on whatever flavours you add. It's an extremely easy process, but you do have to think about it in advance, as you need to soak the cashews overnight. As with similar recipes, be careful to stop and start your blender so as not to overwork the motor. The cream will keep for a few days once refrigerated.

150g/5½oz/1 cup raw cashews, soaked overnight or for a minimum of 8 hours

**For sour cream**

a dash of apple cider vinegar

a dash of olive oil

a squeeze of lemon

1 tsp onion powder

salt and pepper to taste

**For sweet cream**

1 tbsp agave syrup
(more if you like it sweeter)

½ tsp vanilla extract

**1** To make either version, simply drain the cashews, then put everything in a blender, adding water as needed, and blend to a creamy consistency. Season the sour variation to taste before serving.

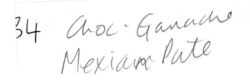

34  Choc. Ganache
Mexican Pate

...d – we tend just to put everything ...eady in the morning – this is a quick ...r about three days once made. It's ...or with raw crackers or even in a ...ut keeping the whole thing raw. ...res and it adds such depth to this ...'s a great ingredient to discover

...e ..., soaked • ...g/3¾oz/1 cup sunflower seeds, soaked • 75g/2¾oz/½ cup walnuts, soaked • ½ small red onion, roughly chopped • 1 tomato, roughly chopped • a handful of fresh coriander (cilantro) leaves • a handful of fresh flat-leaf parsley • 1 tsp brown rice miso • 1 yellow pepper, deseeded and roughly chopped • a pinch of ground cumin • ½ garlic clove • a handful of sun-dried tomatoes, roughly chopped • ½ chipotle chilli, soaked

Blend everything together in food processor, adding a little water if necessary to achieve a well-mixed pâté that still has a little texture.

# Walnut pâté

60g/2¼/½ cup walnuts, soaked overnight (minimum of 8 hours) • 55g/2oz/1 cup sun-dried tomatoes, soaked for about an hour • ½ tsp brown rice miso • 2 tsp dried oregano • 1 tsp tamari (make sure it's gluten free) • ½ tsp cayenne • 2 tbsp olive oil • 1 tsp agave syrup

Blend everything in a food processor, to achieve a well-mixed pâté with a slightly chunky texture.

# Carrot kinpira

SERVES 4
WF | GF

Popular in bento boxes, this is another tasty Japanese side dish that we often serve as a little extra with our meals or as part of a sharing meal made up of lots of little bits and pieces. One of our real favourites is a simple meal combining this kinpira with brown rice, Maple-glazed Tofu (p.117) and maybe a few greens or a Miso Soup (p.33). Already combining sweet and savoury, the addition of the arame also adds to the mix the elusive umami, one of the five basic tastes (the others being sweet, sour, salty, bitter) that really deepens the flavour profile of all it touches!

1 tbsp coconut oil (or cooking oil of your choice)

4 carrots, peeled and cut into batons

2 tbsp dried arame, rehydrated in water

1 tbsp mirin

1 tbsp toasted sesame oil

2 tbsp tamari (make sure it's gluten free)

a pinch of dried red chilli flakes

1 tbsp white sesame seeds

**1** Heat the coconut oil in a wok before adding the carrots. Cook on a high heat for 4–5 minutes until they've taken on a nice bit of colour.

**2** Add the arame and mirin and cook for a further minute or so before adding the sesame oil, tamari and chilli flakes. Cook for a final 30 seconds, then sprinkle in the sesame seeds.

**3** Serve hot or cold.

# Carrot and kimchi pickle

SERVES 4
WF | GF

This is how we use Kimchi in our signature Buddha Bowls (p.116), but it's also a delicious accompaniment to many other things. We use it as a side dish with our curries, but it's lovely inside a wrap, with baked potatoes or with tacos. The pickle-juice part of the recipe makes a decent-sized batch that can be kept for months in a jar in the fridge for future use.

**For the pickle juice**

125ml/4fl oz/½ cup apple cider vinegar

6 tbsp soft brown sugar

1 star anise

3 black peppercorns

a pinch of salt

**For the rest**

4 carrots, grated

125g/4½oz Kimchi (p.146), the average amount a Korean eats in a day!

**1** Put all the pickle-juice ingredients in a pan and bring to the boil, stirring occasionally to ensure the sugar doesn't burn on the bottom. Remove from the heat and leave to cool. Once cool, put in a storage jar in the fridge.

**2** Combine the grated carrot with the Kimchi. Spoon approximately 4 tbsp of the pickle juice over the carrot mixture and leave it to pickle for about an hour, then serve.

# Kimchi

MAKES
1.5L/34FLOZ
/1½ QUARTS
WF | GF
RAW

We love kimchi! This fermented-cabbage side dish is the national dish of Korea and is still a vital part of Korean lifestyle – and indeed, of our Buddha Bowls! It's so important to the nation's culture that Koreans say 'kimchi' instead of 'cheese' when posing for photographs, and it can be served with just about anything, from tacos to Thai curries – experiment! There are many different varieties of kimchi and just as many methods of preparation. Traditionally, kimchi was fermented in stone jars underground for months at a time and generally uses fish sauce and anchovy paste. We've reduced the timings somewhat, made it vegan and just ferment ours in a bucket in a garage, so this is not one for traditionalists, but it's definitely delicious. And because it's fermented, it's great for the immune system and digestion. But whatever you do, it probably is best to keep it somewhere a bit out of the way. It's very smelly!

1 litre/34fl oz/1 quart water

3 tbsp sea salt

1 Chinese leaf (Chinese cabbage)

½ daikon or 6 radishes

1 carrot

2 onions, ½ leek or 6 spring onions (scallions)

45g/1½oz fresh root ginger, peeled and chopped

3 garlic cloves

6 long red chillies, deseeded (use as much or as little as you prefer)

**You'll also need**

sandwich bag

large glass jar for fermenting

**1** Mix the water and salt in a large bowl to make a brine. Stir to dissolve the salt.

**2** Coarsely chop the cabbage and slice the radish, carrot and onions, then soak these vegetables in the brine, using a plate to keep them submerged, until they're soft. This should take about 12 hours.

**3** Just before the vegetables are ready, put the ginger, garlic and chilli in a food processor and blend together to form a rough paste.

**4** Once soft, drain the vegetables but reserve half of the brine. Check how salty they are. If it's too much, give them a rinse; if not salty enough, add some more.

**5** Mix the vegetables with the spice paste and stuff into a sealable jar, leaving some space at the top. Pour some of the reserved brine into a sandwich bag, seal it and put it into the top of the jar to keep the vegetables submerged in the spicy brine. This prevents them from going off.

**6** Seal, then leave to ferment in the kitchen or any cool spot away from sunlight. Taste every couple of days. When it's a little bit fizzy and really delicious, usually after about a week, remove the brine bag and transfer the jar to the fridge, where it will last for at least a couple of weeks.

# Sauerkraut

Like Kimchi (p.146), sauerkraut is a popular fermented-cabbage side dish. Directly translated from German as 'sour cabbage', sauerkraut is finely chopped or grated cabbage that is layered with salt and left to ferment. Once fully cured, it has a wonderful shelf life; kept in an airtight container it can last for weeks. Its health benefits are huge: the fibre, probiotics and enzymes greatly help to improve and protect the digestive system. In Germany, juniper berries are often added, and not only do they have many digestive benefits of their own, they also work brilliantly in terms of taste! You can make pink sauerkraut by adding red cabbage into the mix.

1 large green cabbage, finely sliced or grated, saving 2 large leaves

1½ tbsp salt, plus 1 tsp

a handful of dried juniper berries

### You'll also need

1 large jar

1 sandwich bag

**1** Sterilize a 3–4 litre (3–4 quart) jar by pouring boiling water in it; place a metal spoon in it before doing so to avoid cracking the glass.

**2** Put the cabbage in a bowl, add the salt and juniper berries and mix. (By adding the salt, the natural water is drawn out of the cabbage by osmosis, and this forms the brine that it's going to ferment in.) Put it in the jar immediately, packing it in tightly and continuously pushing the cabbage down in the jar for a few minutes to really start to release the latent water. Place the 2 reserved leaves on top.

**3** Mix the extra salt with 225ml/8fl oz/1 cup water and pour into the sandwich bag. Seal the bag, then put it into the jar to push the cabbage down before sealing the jar.

**4** Store the jar away from direct sunlight. Within 24 hours, you should be able to see the natural brine rising above the cabbage. If it isn't, top up the brine by mixing another batch of water and salt and add that to the jar. The process will take 4–10 days, depending on the weather. Taste the sauerkraut every day; it will have a slightly fizzy but delicious flavour when it's ready. Once it has fermented properly, transfer to the fridge and store until needed. It will keep for 3 weeks or longer.

# Kale crisps

SERVES 2
WF | GF | RAW
OPTION

There's no doubt that kale crisps have played a huge role in the incredible surge of popularity this leafy green has recently enjoyed. And for good reason: these crisps are packed full of the good stuff and are extremely delicious. They're also addictive and cost a fortune bought from health-food stores, but try this and you'll see how easy it is to make your own. We give a raw recipe below to maximize the nutritional benefits, but it does need a dehydrator. Don't worry if you don't have one, though; you can also make a roasted version in the oven, which is still healthy and tastes great. Experiment with different ingredients – this is our classic version, but you can use so many other flavourings - raw cacao powder, smoked paprika, chilli – whatever you fancy! If you want to save time and make big batches, the crisp will last for up to a week in an airtight container or even longer in vacuum bags.

500g/1lb 2oz kale, stalks removed

75g/2¾oz/1 cup raw desiccated coconut

75g/2¾oz/generous ½ cup flaxseed meal

1 tbsp curry powder

6 tbsp nutritional yeast (make sure it's gluten free)

1 tbsp onion powder

4 tbsp olive oil

a pinch of salt and pepper

**1** Put everything in a bowl and mix until the kale has become shiny, has shrunk slightly and is well-coated with all the other ingredients.

**2** Spread the mix onto Teflex sheets and place in a dehydrator set to 45°C/115°F for about 8 hours, moving them around every couple of hours or so.

**3** To prepare in an oven, preheat your oven to 150°C/300°F/gas mark 2. Spread the kale mixture on a baking sheet and roast for 10–15 minutes, moving it around every now and then and keeping an eye on it to make sure it doesn't burn.

**4** Serve at once, or store in an airtight container for a couple of days.

# Truffle popcorn

SERVES 2
WF | GF

Oh, truffle oil! In a world where so many gourmet items involve animal products, truffles or high-quality truffle oil are our favourite decadences – especially white ones, if you can get them. This is first-class, deluxe, top-of-the-range snacking! And if it seems too indulgent for a night in on the sofa, it's also a really fun canapé that always goes down a treat. This makes enough for two to share over a movie.

100ml/3½fl oz/scant ½ cup sunflower oil

250g/9oz/2¼ cups popping corn (popcorn)

2 tbsp white truffle oil

2 tbsp nutritional yeast (make sure it's gluten free)

salt and pepper

1 sprig fresh rosemary, leaves only, finely chopped

**1** Using a heavy-based pan with a lid, heat the sunflower oil over a medium heat before putting 2–3 of the popcorn kernels in the pan and covering with a lid. When the kernels pop, add the rest of the popcorn and turn off the heat. Leave for about 30 seconds before turning the heat back on. At this point, the popcorn should start to pop!

**2** Once it has got going, gently shake the pan backwards and forwards with the lid slightly open to release any built-up steam. When the popping slows down, remove from the heat and transfer the popcorn to a large bowl.

**3** Immediately season with all the other ingredients, mix well and serve.

SERVES 2
WF | GF
RAW
OPTION

# Tamari nuts and seeds

Easy to make (although you need to plan in advance) and probably our favourite snack, these are something we make all the time with whatever nuts or seeds we have to hand. We also use them so often as a tasty sprinkle that not only adds flavour and crunch to any dish but also protein and essential fatty acids, among other things. If you have a dehydrator, the raw version really amps up the nutritional benefits as a result of the germination process, but it's still a very healthy addition if you've used an oven and roasted the nuts and seeds instead. They store in an airtight jar for a month or so.

6 tbsp tamari (make sure it's gluten free)

1 tbsp + 2 tsp agave or sweetener of your choice

500g/1lb 2oz/3⅓ cups mixed seeds, soaked for 8 hours, strained and rinsed (omit the soaking if preparing the roasted version)

1 tbsp chopped fresh herbs of your choice (optional)

**1** Mix the tamari and agave in a bowl before adding the nuts and seeds. Cover the bowl with clingfilm (plastic wrap) and leave it to marinate in the fridge for about 8 hours.

**2** For the raw version, set your dehydrator to 45°C/115°F, spread the marinated nuts and seeds on a Teflex sheet and dehydrate for about 48 hours, moving them around occasionally. Leave to cool, then transfer to an airtight container.

**3** For the roasted version, preheat the oven to 180°C/350°F/gas mark 4. Put the nuts and seeds on a baking sheet and roast for 15–20 minutes until golden, watching closely and moving them around to prevent them from burning.

**4** Leave to cool, then transfer to an airtight container.

# Powerballs

We love it when nutrition-packed raw food is also extremely easy to make and these powerballs really fit that bill. They can be ready in less than 5 minutes and will keep for about 5 days in the fridge in an airtight container. That being said, to maximize the nutritional benefits you could also try soaking the seeds for about 8 hours to germinate them. You then just drain them and carry on as per the recipe. Great as a snack or for taking with you on the go, these are one of our staples. As ever, experiment as much as you like with different fillings and coatings. Any superfood powders, wonder seeds or magical fruits will work perfectly.

100g/3½oz/⅔ cup pumpkin or sunflower seeds

4 tbsp sesame seeds, plus a bit extra for rolling

50g/1¾oz/⅔ cup desiccated coconut (plus a bit extra for rolling)

2 tbsp ground flaxseed

50g/1¾oz/⅓ cup dried fruit mix (dates, apricots, raisins)

1–2 tbsp of your favourite superfoods, such as lacuma or maca

50g/1¾oz cacao nibs

1 tsp ground cinnamon, plus extra for rolling

raw cacao powder, for rolling (optional)

125ml/4fl oz/½ cup maple or agave syrup, or sweetener of your choice

80g/2¾oz/⅓ cup nut or seed butter – just make sure it's raw

a pinch of sea salt

**1** Combine all ingredients except the maple syrup, nut butter and salt in a food processor, and pulse until well mixed. Add the remaining ingredients and continue to blend until the mixture has started to become smooth but still has some texture.

**2** With your hands, roll the mixture into bite-sized pieces about the size of ping pong balls. Put extra cinnamon, sesame seeds, coconut and cacao, if using, into separate bowls and then, so you have a selection, roll a few of the powerballs into each one to coat. Eat immediately or store in the fridge in an airtight container for future snacking.

DRINKS &
SMOOTHIES

# Kombucha

Thought to have been developed in China around 200 years BC and known as the 'immortal health elixir', kombucha is a fizzy, fermented tea that has enormous health benefits that are gaining it a cult following around the globe, especially in the US, where it is on tap at many health-food stores. It's super-rich in many detoxification enzymes and bacterial acids, contains glucosamine, which helps in joint care, and is extremely rich in immune-boosting antioxidants and probiotics that help the digestive system. For your first batch, you'll need a scoby or mushroom, which you can get online or from kombucha-brewing friends. You'll also need some ready-to-go kombucha (from a health-food store) to prevent unfriendly bacteria from growing.

3.5 litres/118fl oz/3½ quarts water

200g/7oz/1 cup white sugar

8 teabags (it's best to use caffeinated tea without essential oils; black tea is good to start with but you can also use green, white or oolong)

500ml/17fl oz/generous 2 cups starter kombucha (store-bought or ideally from your last batch)

1 scoby per jar

flavouring of your choice, such as hibiscus flowers, fruit juice, ginger – experiment!

**You'll also need**

2 x 2-litre/2-quart glass jars, rinsed with boiling water to sanitize them

muslin (cheesecloth) or kitchen towel

2 elastic bands

glass bottles

**1** Boil the water, then remove from the heat and stir in the sugar until dissolved. Add the teabags and leave to brew until the water is cool. Remove the bags and stir in the starter kombucha, then pour into the jars and slide a scoby into each one with clean hands. Cover with muslin or kitchen paper (paper towels) and secure with elastic bands.

**2** Keep away from direct sunlight and leave to ferment at room temperature for 7–10 days, checking occasionally, until the kombucha has a well-balanced flavour (it should have a nice combination of sweet and tart notes).

**3** Remove the scoby from each jar with clean hands, then strain the liquid into glass bottles, leaving some empty space at the top. (This is a good point to make your next batch – simply repeat step one using 500ml/17fl oz/generous 2 cups of your first kombucha haul. You can re-use each scoby every time you make a new batch. If they become too thick over time, just remove their bottom layer. Remember when a scoby goes black or mouldy, it's time to throw it away; they do have a natural lifespan.)

**4** Add a flavouring to the bottles, if you like, then stir well and seal the lids. Store at room temperature away from direct sunlight for 1–3 days to carbonate. When the kombucha is nice and fizzy, strain if necessary and refill the bottles, then transfer the bottles to the fridge to halt the fermentation process. Store chilled for up to 1 month.

While it's easy to buy an array of non-dairy milks, there's something very satisfying about making your own. They'll definitely taste better and are also additive- and preservative-free! A high-speed blender is preferable, but it's possible in a normal blender – just make sure your ingredients are very well soaked and blend in bursts so you don't stress the motor.

# Almond milk

MAKES
1 LITRE/34FL
OZ/1 QUART
WF | GF
RAW

2 handfuls of almonds • 1 litre/34fl oz/1 quart cold, filtered water • a piece of muslin (cheesecloth)

**1** Soak the almonds for at least 8 hours in cold water.

**2** Strain the almonds, transfer to a blender with the water and blend until smooth. Strain the mixture through muslin to separate the almond meal from the milk. (You can use the meal like a flour in a range of cakes and biscuits.) Keep the milk in an airtight container in the fridge for up to 2 days (if it separates, just give it a stir before using).

# Soya milk

MAKES 1
LITRE/34FL
OZ/1 QUART
WF | GF
RAW

200g/7oz/1 cup dry soya beans • water

**1** Rinse the soya beans, then soak in plenty of water for 6 hours.

**2** Drain, then transfer to a saucepan with plenty of fresh water – you don't have to be exact – and bring to the boil. Cover the pan with a lid and continue to boil for 15 minutes, lifting the lid occasionally to release the steam, until the beans are cooked but still have a little bit of a bite.

**3** Drain, then put in a bowl and cover with cold water. Gently roll the beans in your hand and the skins will float to the top of the water. Drain them off and top up with fresh water until all the beans are skinned. Strain once again.

**4** Put the beans and water in a blender and whiz for 1–2 minutes. Strain into an airtight jar and keep for up to 3 days in the fridge.

MAKES 1 LITRE/34FL OZ/1QUART
WF | GF
RAW

# Green antioxidant smoothie

A staple of raw-food diets, this smoothie might not win any prizes for looks, but it packs a mean nutritional punch and it tastes great, too! It's absolutely loaded with antioxidants that help to hoover up the free radicals caused by unhealthy diet and environmental pollutants, all of which are believed to play a role in causing premature ageing as well as heart disease, cancer and many other illnesses. By having a smoothie, as opposed to a juice, you're also keeping all the fibre intact, thereby regulating the flow of sugar and keeping all the digestive benefits of the fibre. The fruit makes it more enjoyable to drink, but can be omitted and replaced with extra green veg, if you prefer, to reduce the sugar content. Either way, it's a really brilliant way to start the day, even more effective than a double espresso! Spirulina, chlorella or blue-green algae can be bought powdered from all good health-food stores.

2 tbsp golden flaxseeds or chia seeds
1 banana
80g/2¾oz pineapple, cut into chunks
1 apple, cored and quartered
65g/2¼oz/heaped 1 cup spinach
65g/2¼oz/1 cup kale
600ml/20fl oz/2½ cups water
1–3 tsp spirulina, chlorella or blue-green algae (optional)
ice (optional)

**1** Put the flaxseeds or chia seeds into a blender and pulse until they form a powder. (Ideally you should use a high-speed blender for this, but any good-quality blender should work fine.)

**2** Put everything apart from the ice into the blender and mix on a high speed until it is as smooth as possible. Add the ice, if using, and blend again until smooth, then pour into glasses and enjoy straightaway.

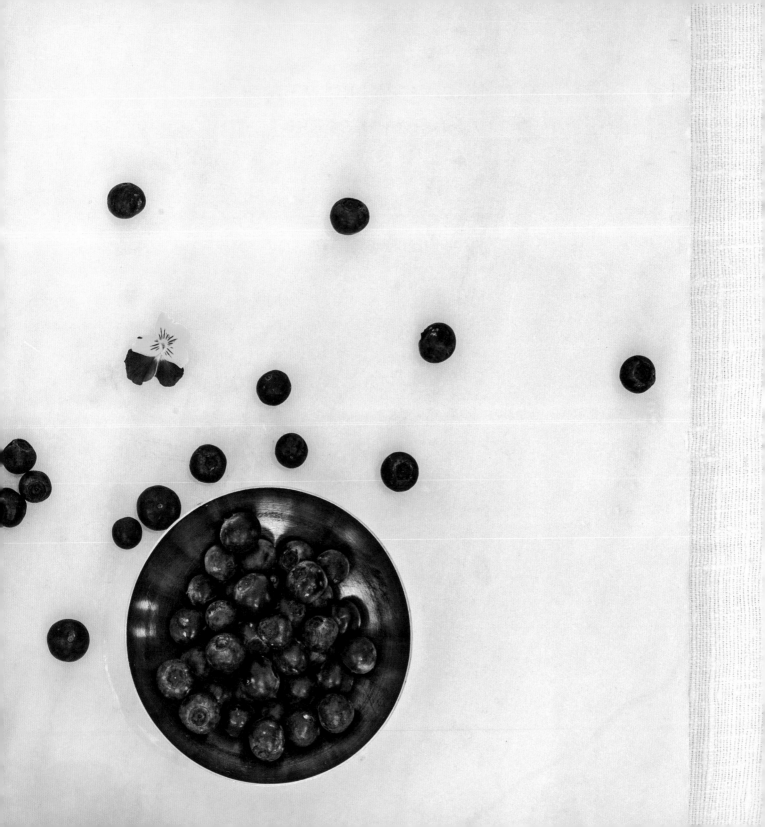

# Blueberry and vanilla antioxidant shake

SERVES 4
WF | GF | RAW

A wonderful breakfast drink, this shake is a really tasty treat that is also extremely good for you. The blueberries, maple, lacuma (a natural sweetener derived from the Peruvian lacuma fruit) and chia seeds are all superfoods and are extremely rich in antioxidants to protect against free-radical damage, as well as having many other health benefits. Both lacuma and chia can be easily bought online or from health-food stores.

1 batch Almond Milk, homemade (p.157) or store-bought • 250g/9oz blueberries/generous 1½ cups • ½ chopped banana • 4 tbsp maple syrup • ¼ tsp vanilla extract • 1 apple, cored • 1 cup crushed ice • 2 tbsp lacuma powder • 1 tbsp chia seeds

Put everything in a blender and blend to combine. Taste as you go and adjust the sweeteners and vanilla to your preference.

# Chocolate 'milk'

SERVES 4
WF | GF | RAW

A treat for grown-ups or a way to get kids interested in raw food – raw cacao is one of the world's top superfoods, being rich in vitamins, minerals (it's the richest edible food source of magnesium), fibre and essential fatty acids. Maca also boasts a wide range of nutrients. Obtained from a Peruvian root, it can be a bit of an acquired taste, but you'll soon be hooked! This drink gives you a good energy boost, so it's great when you need a bit of pepping up. You can find raw cacao powder and maca online or in health-food stores.

600ml/20fl oz/2½ cups cold Almond Milk, homemade (p.157) or store-bought • 4 tbsp raw cacao powder • 2 tbsp carob powder • 1 tsp maca • 4 tbsp agave syrup • 1 cup of ice

Simply put everything in a blender and combine. Adjust the sweetener, cacao and maca to your personal preference.

MAKES
1 LITRE/34FL
OZ/1 QUART
WF | GF
RAW

# Homemade lemonade with chia seeds

This super-refreshing drink reminds us of happy, sunny days on the beach in Mexico, where the wonder seed chia, much-beloved by the Mayans, is liberally added to most things. As well as being jam-packed with good nutrition, chia seeds also absorb 10 times their weight in water, so they form a kind of bulky gel when added to liquids that really helps hydration on long, sticky days. Many long-distance cyclists add them to their water bottles to take advantage of this; also the gel helps make you feel full. As a source of omega-3 oils, we find them much more user-friendly than flaxseed as they're far easier to digest and don't need to be ground. This is an all-round winner for summer barbecues or picnics.

5 unwaxed lemons, peeled and roughly chopped, (reserving the zest of 1)

150ml/5fl oz/scant ⅔ cup agave syrup

1 litre/34fl oz/1 quart cold water

8 sprigs fresh mint to garnish, plus extra to garnish

ice

2 tbsp chia seeds

**1** Put the lemons, lemon zest, agave and water in a blender and combine on high speed for about a minute. Add the mint and blend for a further 10 seconds.

**2** Put a few ice cubes in each glass, top with the lemonade and stir in 1–2 tsp of the chia seeds. Leave for a few minutes to allow the chia to soak a little, then garnish each glass with a sprig of mint. and serve.

BASICS

# Sprouting

A handful or two of raw sprouts added to a meal is one of the easiest and most powerful ways to boost its nutritional content. The process of soaking and rinsing removes enzyme inhibitors and begins the germination process whereby all the latent nutrition in the seeds breaks down into simple components – much easier for the body to digest. Plus, the nutrient content multiplies as the seeds get ready to become fully fledged plants – they truly are living foods! Most health-food stores sell sprouting jars, but you can also make your own using a jam jar with holes punched in the lid. We find it's best to sprout one type of seed at a time. Experiment with different varieties; we mostly use mung beans, sunflower seeds, chickpeas, lentils, quinoa and alfalfa. A word of warning: the germination process can lead to dangerous bacterial growth, so follow the instructions carefully.

80–100g/3–3½oz/½–⅔ cup seeds of your choice **You'll also need** 1 sprouting jar, or jam jar with holes poked in the lid and some muslin to place between the jar and the lid

**1** Put the seeds in the jar and cover with water before giving them a good mix. Drain. Fill again with water and leave to soak for about 8 hours.

**2** Drain the water, rinse with fresh water, then leave the jar – on its side so that air can circulate – for 2–4 days, depending on the sprouts. They should be 1–2cm/½–¾in when ready. Rinse them 2–3 times a day during this process. Once they've sprouted, give them a good rinse, drain, then put them in a sealed container in the fridge for a maximum of 2 days.

# Basic raw salad dressing

250ml/9fl oz/1 cup + 2 tbsp cold-pressed olive oil • 125ml/4fl oz/½ cup lemon juice • 2 dates, pitted

Simply blend all the ingredients together. Use immediately.

# Raw mexican dressing

SERVES 4
WF | GF | RAW

1 batch of Basic Raw Salad Dressing (above) • ½ bunch fresh coriander (cilantro) • ¼ bunch of fresh parsley • 1 garlic clove, chopped • 1 red chilli, deseeded and chopped • zest and juice of 1 lime • 1½ tbsp ground cumin • 2 tomatoes • 1 avocado, peeled and stoned

Put all the ingredients, except the avocado, in a blender and blend until smooth. Add the avocado and blend again. Use immediately.

# Raw sesame dressing

SERVES 4
WF | GF | RAW

1 garlic clove, roughly chopped • a pinch of salt • juice of 1 lemon • 2 tbsp raw tahini (from a well-stirred jar!) • 2 tbsp olive oil

Put all the ingredients in a blender and blend until smooth, adding a little water to aid you as you go, but keeping the dressing fairly thick. The dressing will last for a couple of days in the fridge.

# Green pesto

SERVES 4
WF | GF | RAW

1 bunch of fresh basil • ½ bunch of fresh flat-leaf parsley • 1 garlic clove • a handful of raw pine nuts • 2½ tbsp olive oil • salt and pepper

Blend all the ingredients in a blender or food processor, adding olive oil as desired. The pesto should be quite dry. Use within 24 hours.

# Aioli

SERVES 4
WF | GF

1 garlic bulb • a drizzle of olive oil • 150g/5½oz/⅔ cup vegan mayonnaise • 10 strands saffron, soaked in 2 tbsp water

Preheat the oven to 180°C/350°F/gas mark 4. Cut the garlic bulb in half horizontally, drizzle it generously with olive oil and put it on a baking sheet to roast for about 15 minutes. Remove the roasted garlic cloves from their shells – they should just fall out – and crush in a pestle and mortar. Put the vegan mayonnaise in a bowl and mix in the roasted garlic, saffron strands and their soaking water, and mix to form a thick sauce. The aioli can be stored in the fridge for 4–6 days.

# Miso dipping sauce

SERVES 4
WF | GF

75ml/2½fl oz/5 tbsp sake • 50ml/1⅔fl oz/3½ tbsp mirin • 100g/3½oz/½ cup sugar • 225g/½lb white miso paste (sometimes known as sweet)

Mix the sake and mirin in a saucepan and flambé over a high heat to burn off the alcohol. Add the sugar and whisk until dissolved. Bring to the boil, then reduce the heat to low, add the miso and whisk until combined. Remove from the heat and leave to cool. The sauce can be stored in the fridge for 5–7 days.

# Sweet chilli dipping sauce

SERVES 4
WF | GF

120g/4½oz/⅔ cup brown sugar • 2 long red chillies, deseeded • 2 garlic cloves •125ml/4fl oz/ ½ cup rice wine vinegar • a pinch of salt • 2 kaffir lime leaves (optional)

Put all the ingredients, except the lime leaves, in a pan and bring to the boil. Remove from the heat, transfer to a blender and pulse until well combined. Return the pan to the heat and add the lime leaves. Bring back to the boil and simmer until thickened. Leave to cool. The sauce can be stored in the fridge for up to 1 month.

# Marinara sauce

SERVES 4
WF | GF | RAW

115g/4oz/2 cups sun-dried tomatoes, soaked for about 1 hour • 4 plum tomatoes, seeded and chopped • 12 cherry tomatoes • 1 garlic clove, peeled • ½ tsp salt • 1 tbsp chopped shallots (green onions) • 3 tbsp olive oil • 2 tbsp maple syrup • ½ tsp lemon juice • 8 fresh basil leaves • 2 tbsp dried oregano • 1½ tsp fresh thyme leaves

Put the sun-dried tomatoes in a blender and process until they are in small pieces. Add the plum and cherry tomatoes, garlic, salt, shallots, olive oil, maple syrup and lemon juice and process until smooth. Add the basil, oregano and thyme and pulse until all the herbs are chopped. Use immediately.

# Tartare sauce

SERVES 4
WF | GF

½ jar vegan mayonnaise • 2 tbsp capers, rinsed • 1 gherkin, chopped • ½ shallot, chopped • 1 tbsp chopped fresh dill • a twist of lemon

Simply mix all the ingredients together and chill until ready to serve. The sauce can be stored in the fridge for up to 2 days.

# Asian vegetable stock

MAKES
2.5L/87½FL OZ
12 CUPS
WF | GF

12 dried shiitake mushrooms • 3 carrot, roughly chopped • 6 spring onions (scallions), roughly chopped • 1 tsp salt • 1 tsp tamari (make sure it's gluten free) • 30g/1oz fresh root ginger, peeled and roughly chopped • 1 celery stick, roughly chopped • 1 onion, roughly chopped • 3 litres/102fl oz/3 quarts water•

Put all the stock ingredients in a large pan and bring to the boil. Simmer for 30 minutes, then strain and set aside, reserving the shiitake mushrooms if necessary.

# Vegetable stock

MAKES
2L/60FL OZ/
2 QUARTS
WF | GF

1 tbsp vegetable oil • 1 carrot, roughly chopped • 1 onion, 1 leek, 4 sticks celery, 1 tomato and 4 button mushrooms, all roughly chopped • 10g/¼oz fresh herbs (rosemary, parsley, thyme, or a mix) • 1 bay leaf • a pinch of salt • 5 black peppercorns

Heat the oil, then sauté the vegetables for 5 minutes on a high heat. Add 3 litres/102fl oz/3 quarts water, the herbs, bay leaf, salt and peppercorns and simmer gently for 20–30 minutes. Strain into a large bowl and allow to cool.

# Laksa vegetable stock

MAKES
2L/60FL OZ/
2 QUARTS
WF | GF

1 onion, chopped • 1 carrot, chopped • 30g/1oz fresh root ginger, peeled and sliced • ½ bunch of spring onions (scallions), chopped • 2–3 dried shiitake mushrooms • ½ bunch of fresh flat-leaf parsley • ½ bunch of fresh coriander (cilantro) • 2 garlic cloves, sliced in half • 2 litres/68fl oz/2 quarts water • salt and pepper

Put all the ingredients in a large pan. Add a pinch of salt and pepper and bring to the boil, then reduce the heat and leave to simmer. After 30 minutes, strain the stock into a bowl, discarding the solids, and use as required.

# Laksa curry paste

SERVES 4
WF | GF

1 tbsp coriander seeds • 100g/3½oz shallots (green onions), chopped • 2 garlic cloves, chopped • 30g/1oz fresh root ginger, peeled and chopped • 2 sticks lemongrass, finely chopped • 4 dried red chillies, deseeded and chopped • 50g/2oz fresh coriander (cilantro), chopped • 1 tbsp medium curry powder (make sure it's gluten free)

To make the paste, lightly toast the coriander seeds in a dry frying pan over a low heat for 1–2 minutes until fragrant. Grind the toasted seeds in a pestle and mortar, then transfer to a blender or food processor with a pinch of salt and pepper and all the remaining paste ingredients and pulse until smooth.

# Massaman curry paste

SERVES 4
WF | GF

1 tbsp vegetable oil • 1–2 sticks lemongrass, chopped • 5 garlic cloves, chopped • 2 tbsp peeled and chopped galangal • 5 dried long, red chillies, deseeded, soaked in water and drained • 2 tbsp chopped fresh coriander (cilantro) root • 6 shallots (green onions), chopped • 2 cloves • 1 tbsp coriander seeds • 6 black peppercorns • ½ cinnamon stick • 2 cardamom pods • 1 tsp ground cumin • ¼ nutmeg, freshly grated • a large pinch of salt • 2 tbsp roasted peanuts

Put the oil in a wok on full heat, add the lemongrass, garlic, galangal, chillies, coriander root, shallots and a splash of water. Fry until golden, stirring occasionally and adding a little more water if the pan is getting dry. Once golden, transfer to a blender. Add the cloves, coriander seeds, peppercorns, cinnamon and cardamom to the wok and toast for about 20 seconds – don't let them smoke. Add to the blender, then warm the cumin and nutmeg in the hot wok, off the heat, for about 10 seconds. Add to the blender with the salt and peanuts and blend until smooth.

# Thai green curry paste

SERVES 4
WF | GF

40g/1½oz garlic, roughly chopped • 80g/3oz/½ cup white onion, roughly chopped • 2 sticks lemongrass, roughly chopped • 25g/1oz galangal, peeled and roughly chopped • 50g/1¾oz long green chillies, deseeded and roughly chopped • 5g/⅙oz green bird's-eye chilli, deseeded and roughly chopped • 3 kaffir lime leaves • ½ bunch of fresh coriander roots; keep the leaves for later and for garnish • a pinch of roughly chopped fresh or ground turmeric

Put all the ingredients in a food processor and blitz to a smooth paste.

# Nasi goreng paste

SERVES 4
WF | GF

¼ nutmeg, freshly grated • ¾ tsp black peppercorns • 30g/1oz shallots (green onions), finely chopped • 15g/½oz fresh root ginger, peeled and finely chopped • 20g/¾oz galangal, peeled and finely chopped • ½ knob turmeric, finely chopped • 1½ sticks lemongrass, chopped • 2 garlic cloves, finely chopped • 1 red chilli, deseeded and finely chopped • 1½ tsp palm sugar • a pinch of salt • 1½ tbsp coconut oil • juice of ½ lime

Put all the ingredients in a food processor and blitz to a smooth paste.

SERVES 2

# Seitan

First developed in China as a meat substitute for vegetarian Buddhist monks, seitan, or wheat gluten as it's otherwise known, is made by washing wheat flour to separate the gluten from the starch. It is hugely popular throughout Asia, especially for making mock duck, and much-embraced in the US, but for some reason it isn't commonly used in the UK. This is a shame, as it's easy and fun to make yourself, and if you're looking for a meat substitute, its chewy, sinewy texture is a much closer match than the soy options of tofu and tempeh.

500g/1lb 2oz/4 cups strong white flour (bread flour)

a little oil to grease

**1** Put the flour in a bowl and gradually mix in small amounts of water until you have a firm dough. Knead for 5 minutes, then transfer to an oiled bowl. Cover and leave in the fridge for at least 4 hours or, preferably, overnight.

**2** When it's ready, uncover the dough and place the bowl in the sink. Under cold running water, gently knead the dough with your fingertips; try to keep it submerged while you're kneading, and allow the cloudy water to run over the top of the bowl – this is the starch leaving the dough. Continue kneading for 15–20 minutes until the water runs clear and you're left with a much smaller piece of sinewy, elastic dough. Use as directed in the recipe.

# Index

We're so very grateful to so many people, but first thanks have to go to Mama/Miranda, the vegetarian trailblazer of this family and all-round inspiration to us all. I might have complained about all that healthy food as a kid but you were right as usual and we get it now. We're eternally grateful for your boundless love and support.

And to Dad/Michael, for braving the depths of the Wing Yip cash and carry when we ran out of stock, and for being the only one brave enough to drive the H van on her maiden voyage! Knowing you've been behind us every step of the way has meant more than you could ever know.

Of course we're so grateful to the lovely team at Pavilion who have enabled this book to happen and put in so many hours of work. To Becca, Fiona, Krissy, Zoe and Kom – it's been such a wonderful opportunity and process and we're so thrilled with the result. Thank you! We also owe huge thanks to the photographic geniuses Liz and Max Haarala, and also to the wonderful food stylist Sara Lewis. The photos are just fantastic and make us hungry every time we look at them!

An enormous thank you to all our friends and family who have supported and encouraged us in so many ways and at so many events come rain or shine. Especial thanks to Ellie and also to Kev and Taryn, who braved 18-hour days and the risk of trench foot to help us through some of our first jobs.

And finally, thank you to our lovely Buddha Bowl customers for giving our business its life.

David & Charlotte Bailey

First published in paperback in the United Kingdom in 2018 by Pavilion
43 Great Ormond Street, London WC1N 3HZ

ISBN: 978-1-911624-07-3

A CIP catalogue record for this book is available from the British Library

10 9 8 7 6 5 4 3 2 1

Reproduction by Mission Productions Ltd, Hong Kong
Printed and bound by 1010 Printing International Ltd, China

This book can be ordered direct from the publisher at www.pavilionbooks.com